FREE OFFER

As a gift to readers of my book, I am giving away a free copy of my e-book *21 Things You Didn't Know About Power*.

https://www.natashaoquendo.com/free-gift

You are Powerful!
Love,
Natasha
Oquendo

INVITATION 2 QUEENDOM

INVITATION 2 QUEENDOM

7 KEYS TO UNLOCK YOUR
GOD-GIVEN SUPERPOWER

NATASHA
OQUENDO

DEDICATION

To all my wonderful readers around the world, I decree
Freedom, in knowing that GOD empowers women!

CONTENTS

INTRODUCTION

Since the age of nineteen years old there has been a calling on my life to help women. I had no idea it would become one of my God-given assignments, but it definitely became a reality in my late twenties. I remember feeling a bit nervous in the beginning about volunteering at the women's prison, but I can honestly say that it was one of the most powerful decisions I could have ever made concerning ministry. I had been going back and forth to the prison, but this particular visit was different.

I was twenty-nine years old. It was a Friday evening and as I was driving to the prison, I felt this strong sense of urgency to pray against the spirit of suicide. I remember parking my car in the prison parking lot and still being unable to stop praying. As I stepped out of my vehicle and my feet hit the ground, I saw a vision. In the vision, there was this massive cloud moving over the prison as I was walking up to the door and moving through the process of checking in. Now mind you, I saw myself in this vision, and I was extremely small, but the cloud was overpowering. I was still praying under my breath saying, "You, stronghold of suicide, I pull you down," and because I was caught up in prayer, I was running a few minutes late.

I walked through the compound still repeating that prayer, and just as I stepped over the threshold of the prison sanctuary, I heard the woman who was doing the opening prayer say, "God said, the stronghold of suicide that was hovering over the prison has been broken."

I remember sitting down just full of gratitude towards God as I listened to the woman share that three women in the prison had committed suicide that week. As the service went forth and we ministered to the women and laid hands on them, there was a powerful move of God in that service. At the end of the service is when it happened. One of the inmates whom I had prayed for came up to me and fell into my arms crying and said, "I look for you every time because it's like you bring God here with you."

At that moment I felt the weight of my assignment from God. As I walked through the compound to leave that evening, I couldn't help but notice the loud clang of the bars closing behind me. Now, I had heard this sound many times before, but this time there was a distinct difference in my sensitivity to the loud slam. In that instance, I knew that it was a sound that I would never forget.

During my ride home, the Lord began to show me how I could have been in prison myself and how He had preserved my life. Then He went into how many of us as women who were free in fact were still in prison in our minds, emotions, and lives. He showed me that He had given me the keys to release them from bondage, just as He had released me, and that the appointed time was coming when a mighty move of God would take place among women. It was some time after this life-changing encounter that I completed my studies with a bachelor's degree in ministry.

I have been afforded various opportunities to impact the lives of women, ministering and volunteering in women's prisons, homeless and abuse shelters, chemical addiction recovery centers, local high schools, women's conferences, radio, and media ministry. After many years of providing spiritual wisdom, guidance, and consultation in the areas of life, marriage, ministry, and personal development, the Lord sanctioned me to write this book.

I remember being in church one day thinking, "Man, this is totally not what I expected it to be." No one prepared me for the various things I would experience. Yes, there were other women who had been in the faith longer than me, but they, themselves, were fighting to keep their head above water, and many were literally drowning in their effort; to the point that I thought you were supposed to drown somewhere along the way. Now, after almost drowning, I've made it to the other side called understanding. It is my heart's desire that we as women of faith have the ability to accurately identify where we are in our walk, break the bondage of stagnation in our lives, and unlock the power to move forward without aborting the sincerity of our belief in God.

Although I have done diverse areas of ministry and impacted the lives of women spiritually and naturally, one of the main objectives of my purpose is to be a noble manifestation of God's power in, to, and through women. To let you know that it is time to move to your next level. That it's time to know your God-given identity. To take your rightful position and to function at the level of authority that God has given you. Yes, you can do this!

Within these pages are a wealth of wisdom, understanding, and knowledge vital for you to evolve into the spiritually healthy woman of God you were designed and destined to be.

Chapter 1 introduces the foundation that God himself is the true source to understanding our position as women. Expressive of this fact is that we were equally included in the promises and that we are needed to help bring those promises to fulfillment.

Chapter 2 addresses various emotional hang-ups many of us face as women and how to get to the place of true freedom.

Chapter 3 explores our experiences with men in relationships and how those past relationships affect our present and future relationships.

Chapter 4 journeys through the fundamentals of what it really means to be made whole as a woman of faith.

Chapter 5 addresses all things pertaining to being a daughter. From the natural daughter, to becoming a daughter of the faith, to evolving into a spiritual daughter. This chapter also touches on the somewhat controversial topic of having spiritual parents.

Chapter 6 gives a breakdown about the powerful gift of serving God. This chapter is the who, what, where, when, why, and how of serving the Lord.

Chapter 7 welcomes us to the realm of favor in God. It speaks of the specific attributes and manifestations that come with functioning in this realm of existence as a queen in the kingdom of God.
When you're done reading this book you will:

- Discover your true God-given identity
- Realize the importance of your position as a woman of faith
- Visibly recognize where you are in your faith and how to advance forward
- Learn how to victoriously break through personal hang -ups
- Gain the ability to access and operate in a level of God's favor that will yield benefits in every area of life: relationships, ministry, and business.

Invitation 2 Queendom is not about being called "queen" as just a mere title, but more about being properly positioned and equipped to function in the realm of your God-given rights. We know all too well that a title alone means nothing without the power to execute its authority. For this to happen, we must be truly awakened to our God-given identity. We must embrace our God-ordained level of class and moral excellence as queens within His kingdom. The world needs you in your rightful God-given position as a Queen, skillfully exercising your realm of existence to assist in the battle to bring "healing to the nations," knowing that the good, the bad, and the ugly of your process is all working uniquely together in your favor. I declare that we are in "The Time of the Woman." Yes, it is your time! Receive your Invitation 2 Queendom.

1ST KEY

BELIEVE
THE
TRUTH

THE SOURCE

IN THE BEGINNING

There is a familiar saying, that if you want to know the truth about something, then you must go to the source. From the very beginning, God had a wonderful layout for the creation of mankind. I would like to take this time to revert to His original plan he had set up for us as women. In the book of Genesis, chapter one, as God exercised His creativity by day six, he was mindful to begin his process of creating us, male and female. Genesis 1:26-27 reads:

> *26 Then God said, "Let Us make man in Our image, according to Our likeness; let them have dominion over the fish of the sea, over the birds of the air, and over the cattle, over all the earth and over every creeping thing that creeps on the earth." 27 So God created man in His own image; in the image of God He created him; male and female He created them.*

This is powerful because the Creator Himself laid a foundation for us to truly understand our identity. Woman was also made in the very image of God. This is not only encouraging, but more so a mindset shifter. This is no different than a daughter who looks or acts like her father. The focus here was not put on the male or female aspect, but more so on being created in His image. So, what does it mean to be made in the image of God? Well, John 4:24 says that, "God *is* Spirit, and those who worship Him must worship in spirit and truth."

And He created us with a spirit so that we would have the ability to develop a relationship with Him. There is no diversity there. He created the male and the female together, bearing the image of His spirit so that both of them would be able to connect with Him. Think about this, God said "let us make man in our image and after our likeness." He spoke this as if someone else was there with Him. Let's go just a little more in depth, shall we?

There are three distinct images of God. First, you have God the Father, Jesus the Son, who is referred to as the Word made flesh, then the Holy Spirit. This is the reason God said, "let us" and "our image," because they were there. So, we are made up of spirit, which is the likeness of God the Father; soul, which is what Jesus came to seek and save; and body, which needs the Holy Spirit to help it understand God. So, when you look at the word "image" it means likeness, it means to resemble, and it even means to be a representative of. This was God's perspective and intention. This was a foundation He laid from the beginning of time. We must not only receive it but live up to it.

THE INCLUSION

Now that we have acknowledged God as the Creator, in Genesis, chapter one, He was doing what He does best: creating. Amid this, He spoke some very powerful instructions to the male and female while they were only in spirit form. This was before He brought them onto the earth in physical form. Genesis 1:27-28 reads:

> [27] *So God created man in His own image; in the image of God He created him; male and female He created them.* [28] *Then God blessed them, and God said to them, "Be fruitful and multiply; fill the earth*

and subdue it; have dominion over the fish of the sea, over the birds
of the air, and over every living thing that moves on the earth."

In this text, God gave clear instructions to both the male and female alike while they were in their purest form, which was spirit. First, he created both in His image, then he blessed them both. He told them both to be fruitful (be productive) and to multiply (increase and grow). To replenish meaning (to restore) the earth. To subdue the earth, which means to bring it under control. To have dominion meaning (to rule) over every living thing that moves in the earth. This instruction, or should I say command, from God was solid and is still valid. He didn't make any differentiations when He spoke it. He did not speak a separate set of instructions for each individual.

I'm here to let you know that as a woman you have every right to embrace the blessings God released. You are a joint heir with equal rights to God's promises of dominion and rulership in the earth. The Creator Himself originally designed it to be this way. The powerful thing is that no one can change what He said, though many have tried. God did not change His mind about you. You just have to change your mind to receive what He has said concerning you. The Word expresses in Galatians 3:28-29:

> *28 There is neither Jew nor Greek, there is neither slave nor free,*
> *there is neither male nor female; for you are all one in Christ*
> *Jesus. 29 And if you are Christ's, then you are Abraham's seed,*
> *and heirs according to the promise.*

So, the promise is yours without stipulations because you are a female. God spoke this before you were born into physical existence; before you even knew or acknowledged Him. These words of prophecy were in play before you knew your identity. Our gender was never designated or intended by God to become this massive issue that us in human form have made it out to be. As a woman it is truly important that we understand it from God's pure perspective. That begins by letting go of everything that has corrupted our thinking and view of ourselves. Let go of past mistakes and failures. Receive and act upon His instructions to you. Woman, you are blessed!

YOU ARE NEEDED

This is a man's world, the view and mindset that rules the atmosphere. Therefore, it is vital that as a woman, you come to realize your importance in this world, as well. God had an original design and intention for creating woman. This knowledge is valuable in a world where the very existence as a female has been diminished to just about one of the lowest positions in the land. To the point that sex trafficking of women and girls, which is simply a form of modern-day slavery, is at an all-time high. Literally, there has been for a very long time an all-out attack against the very existence and position of the woman. But I'm here right now to let you know that we are in "The Time of The Woman!"

You may be wondering, why is she saying this? Let me make myself clear: I don't entertain corrupt feminist movements or men bashing of any kind, for that matter. I have been happily and successfully married to my husband for twenty-one years and together for a total of twenty-three years. I revealed that to say to you that I speak this from a healthy, well-balanced position. I am watching a powerful act of God take place right before my very eyes. God Himself is exalting the woman to her rightful place and position. We saw only small glimpses of this move of God throughout numerous years, but the time we are in now has taken a drastic shift. We saw another glimpse of this grace through First Lady Michelle Obama, and it went a step further with the appointment of Vice President Kamala Harris. These things are not happening just by happenstance; they are manifestations of what God is doing. Not only is God exalting the woman to her rightful position, but He is also vindicating the life and existence of the woman.

We see a major sweeping across the land of those being held accountable for sexual abuse and misconduct committed against women. We see this through the #MeToo movement founded by activist Tarana Burke, which originated to help other women with similar experiences to stand up for themselves. There are various organizations forming to support women against these unlawful acts committed against them. Many states are extending the timeframe of the statues of limitations so that women can report crimes of sexual misconduct committed against them in the past, many that went unreported and unpunished until now. Why? Because this is the time God has chosen to bring these things to account. Why? Because, woman, you are important to God. Not only that, but you hold high importance in the earth. Yes, God brought you into natural existence because you were needed! Genesis 2:18 states: *And the Lord God said, "It is not good that the man should be alone, I will make a helper suitable for him."*

The word "alone" means having no one else present. It also means having no help or participation from others. In other words, mankind could not and still cannot exist properly without you here to help rule it, keep it in order, restore it, increase it, and be productive in it. Neither man nor mankind is blessed without you. I will go into even greater depth about that statement in the next book. As for now, please know that God never intended for you to just be present, but He wanted you to also participate. I say it again: woman you are totally needed!

PREPARED ESPECIALLY FOR YOU

Hopefully, after this we won't be too pumped up with pride (lol) but equipped with a healthy confidence about our identity as women. I noticed something very powerful in Genesis, chapter two. I won't go into certain verses, but in this chapter after God created the heavens, the earth, the seas, etc., He brought the man Adam into existence to work the land and tend to it. He created all the animals and asked Adam to name everything. The Lord saw that there was no suitable help for Adam, so He brought the woman into physical existence. Now, I'm giving a short version of this to make a vital point. God waited until everything was in place before he brought the woman into physical existence. He brought her into an already prepared place. This speaks volumes! Everything was already in its proper place before her arrival. Think about this, it's almost as if she was ushered onto the earth as a queen of some sort. The man God created had to prepare for the woman's arrival.

This scenario coincides with what Jesus spoke to his disciples. He said, "I go to prepare a place for you." The word prepare means to make (someone or something) ready for an activity, purpose, use, etc.

In other words, the world had to be made ready for you. Because you are a woman, God had to make sure everything was prepared for you ahead of time. Whew! If this right here doesn't scream "important" I don't know what does. And let me let you in on a little secret. If you truly believe the words God has spoken and begin to take your rightful position, this could prove to be a way of life for you. I mean, you can live a lifestyle of God, having things prepared for you before you even get on the scene. He ordained you to live in this manner. This is the foundation that was carefully laid for you. When you're really in tune to this, it can prove to be a literal road map to discern the dos and don'ts to what God has especially for you. This is why it is so important as a woman to have patience because people, places, relationships, and things must be made ready for you.

QUEENDOM QUOTE

"A woman who dares to believe
what God has said about her will
stay supplied with the power
to succeed!"

NATASHA OQUENDO

LET'S PRAY...

Father, I thank You for all the wonderful promises
You have established concerning me before
the foundation of the world!
Forgive me for any area of doubt and unbelief!
I declare that it is a new day!
From this day forth, I believe the truth!
I command my life to fully open up to the truth!
I command my mind to embrace the truth!
I am made in Your image!
I am blessed!
My life is productive and filled with positive increase!
I lack no good thing!
I accurately exercise the dominion
you have given me in the earth!
I call forth the things You have
prepared especially for me!
And I decree that signs and wonders
shall follow me because I believe!
In Jesus's name, Amen!

2ND KEY

BE BRAVE
ENOUGH
TO CHANGE!

THE ENCOUNTER

THE ANCIENT ROOT

Now that we are encouraged and becoming aware of our God-given identity and the fact that his intentions for creating us as women is nothing short of amazing, let's take this time to dig a little deeper into where the ancient root of our hang-ups as women began. Though we have heard the story of Adam and Eve various times and told in various ways, I want to take us to the reality of what actually took place in Eve's encounter with the serpent in the Garden of Eden. There are some powerful yet underlying truths that have affected many of our lives as women to this very day. In a nutshell, many of our issues, hang-ups, and dysfunctions were birthed in this one encounter described in Genesis, chapter three. I will break this down in detail to get the full picture. Dissecting this will help us to understand the woman's makeup.

THE SEED OF DOUBT

Be just a little bit patient with me as we take this walk, ladies. Genesis 3:1 (NIV) reads: *Now the serpent was more crafty than any of the wild animals the LORD God had made. He said to the woman, "Did God really say, 'You must not eat from any tree in the garden'?"*

Here we see that the enemy approaches the woman straight off the rip with a question about what God said about the trees in the garden. It's funny that he would choose this particular question, because God actually spoke this specific instruction to Adam before the woman was brought into physical existence.

Genesis 2:16-17 (NIV) states: [16] *And the* LORD *God commanded the man, "You are free to eat from any tree in the garden;* [17] *but you must not eat from the tree of the knowledge of good and evil, for when you eat from it you will certainly die."*

Now, God gave this instruction directly to Adam in verses 16-17. The woman was not brought into physical existence until verse 22. So, this leads me to believe that Adam shared with Eve the command that God gave him about the trees in the garden. Okay, this is a normal way of operating right? A husband shares the information with his wife. But think about this for a minute. Here the enemy shows up to ask the woman a question that she was not physically present to receive the exact answer. She only has the information that Adam passed on to her from God. So, the serpent asks her, "Did God really say you must not eat from every tree in the garden?"

The way this question was asked lets me know that it came with the agenda to plant a seed of doubt. Okay, so did God himself actually say this or did Adam just tell her his version of this? When we look at the word "doubt" it means to feel uncertain or a lack of conviction about what one believes. To disbelieve a person or their word. It also means to question the truth or fact about something. So, by this crafty wordplay the enemy imparted doubt into the mindset of the woman. That may have seemed simple, but look at the extent of what that doubt created by way of these synonyms and let me know if you can honestly identify yourself through some if not all of these. Lack of confidence, lack of trust, confusion, suspicion, skepticism, uneasiness, questioning, and insecurity just to name a few.

Now, if you're anything like me then I'm sure you saw yourself in a few of these. These are the effects that manifested from one seed of doubt being planted. That doubt was the gateway to many of the issues we battle with as women today! Not only do these attributes spring up in our day-to-day lives in various areas and relationships, but the enemy constantly uses these things as weapons against us. Think about how many of us were and still are just outright confused about our position as a woman in this world. We easily have questions and lack true solid understanding of what God has said and intended concerning us.

The entire atmosphere of the world, the church, people, and all other entities have made us feel this sense of skepticism about their interpretation and definition of our purpose, position, and value as women. Many of us live in fear and a lack of confidence because if we're too strong, it's a problem. If we're too soft, it's a problem. Whether were married or single, it's a problem. Have children or remain childless, something's wrong with us. Either our confidence is too low or exaggeratedly too high. The list just goes on and on. There just seems to be no in-between or healthy balance with it all.

My point is that the confusion about women and how we should be is like a thick fog over our lives. No wonder we're having such a hard time grasping and understanding our true identity. All of this derives from one simple statement: "Did God really say…?"

That question was also a test to see if the woman actually knew what God had said. In this very same way as women, we are constantly being tested to see if we not only know but understand what God has said concerning us now.

THE MISCOMMUNICATION

Let's go into the woman's response, shall we? Genesis 3:2-3 reads: The woman said to the serpent, "We may eat fruit from the trees in the garden, but God did say, you must not eat fruit from the tree in the middle of the garden and you must not touch it, or you will die."

Now, this statement is interesting because there was something added to her answer that God did not say. God never said not to touch the tree. He said don't eat the fruit of the tree of knowledge of good and evil. Whether or not Adam added this detail himself when he shared the instructions from God wasn't documented in the scriptures. Maybe he added this detail to ensure that she would take the instruction seriously? Like, look God said just don't so much as touch the tree (lol). Surely, she can't mess nothing up if she doesn't touch it altogether, right? We can only speculate how this went down, but one thing is certain; the instruction from God was definitely miscommunicated and misunderstood. How could something so detrimental be delivered and received without exactness and pinpoint accuracy being that it had life or death attached to it?

"Miscommunicate" means the failure to get a message across clearly. It also means the failure to communicate ideas and intentions successfully. The synonyms are (here we go yet again) confusion, misinterpretation, misconception, misapprehension, mistake, error, and misunderstanding. Are you catching my point? This act of miscommunication caused a grave mistake to be made. This is the very act that is continuing to play itself on repeat in our lives.

What I am saying is that God has said many wonderful and empowering things concerning us as women. But for so long much of what He has said to us and about us has been miscommunicated and we have misinterpreted it, taken on a misconception about it, misunderstood it, and misapprehended it all together, for that matter. Something vital to our wellbeing has been taken out of and added to the message that God himself never intended. These centuries of miscommunication have left us miseducated about ourselves, and it's about time that we were restored and renewed.

THE SENSUAL SIDE

As we move through this piece, I want to bring special attention to a few points. Genesis 3:4-5 reads: *"You will not surely die,"* the serpent said to the woman. *"For God knows that when you eat of it your eyes will be opened, and you will be like God, knowing good and evil."*

Though this is not the key focus, I do want to share it briefly because this is important. If you notice, in these verses the enemy comes off to the woman as if God may have flat-out lied about the dying part. Then he gives the impression that God is withholding some knowledge from her because He doesn't want her to know something to the magnitude that He knows. Though there is some truth in what the enemy said, it's the interpretation he wants to leave her with that's distorted. Although they were not going to die a physical death at this time, the act of disobeying the Lord's instructions caused them to die spiritually. In that spiritual death, they were cut off from the presence of God and access to the Garden of Eden, where they were able to walk and talk with Him. They lost the sensitivity to the spiritual connection they once had the freedom to experience. This one act opened them up to be more sensitive to their flesh and the world around them.

This brings me to my main point in Genesis 3:6 which says: *When the woman saw that the tree was good for food, and that it was pleasing to the eyes, and a tree to be desired to make one wise, she took the fruit and did eat. She also gave some to her husband who was with her, and he did eat.*

Now this was a major transition that took place from being spiritual to becoming sensual. This thing completely changed the course of their intimate relationship and fellowship with God because they were no longer comfortable with God being able to see their nakedness. Which, relating to our modern time, would be to not be able to be transparent with God about who we really are. So much so that when you read on, you see that they withdrew themselves and went into hiding from God. They even sewed together fig leaves as clothing to cover themselves up. This shame got to the point that when God showed up in the Garden, they were afraid when they heard Him coming.

Look how this act ruined a powerful relationship. They had the liberty and freedom to eat from every tree in that garden except for one tree. I'm sure all the fruit on those trees were just as pleasing to the eyes (lol). But that's just like the enemy to make you feel like you're missing out on something that God has said not to do. Let's dig into this. The word sensual means relating to or involving gratification of the senses and physical pleasure. It also means to be devoted to or preoccupied with the senses or bodily appetites. Some synonyms are physical, fleshly, carnal, worldly, sexual, irreligious, and of the human senses. The direct opposite of the word sensual is spiritual. So, by entertaining this encounter with the enemy it opened up extreme sensitivity to the five human senses of natural sight, hearing, smell, taste, and touch. Ladies, this is where the saying "women are so sensitive!" came from. The danger of this is that our feelings can overwhelm us and overpower us to the point that they literally set themselves up as God in our lives. We find ourselves putting our feelings on a pedestal and catering to their every need; forever chasing a good feeling that we can't ever seem to hold onto because feelings are unstable. They are very unreliable. We have literally allowed our feelings to become our discerner of truth and have caused us to hit and miss to the point of getting us into a mess.

To take this a step further, the tree was not only pleasing to the eye, but also desirable to make one wise. Now, the enemy has used this sensualism to entice them to desire wisdom from a source that God told them not to eat from. Minimizing the fact that they were walking and talking to all the wisdom in the world, God Himself, the devil convinced them they could get the wisdom they needed from a tree; making them think they could get something apart from going to God directly for it. Man, this right here is so crucial. Because this is a major part of the problem were facing right now! We have trusted too many sources outside of God to give us the knowledge of our true identity as women and they have failed us miserably. We have allowed every changing fad that the world and the people in it throw our way to define us, leaving us not only incomplete but in a full-fledged identity crisis. Trying to fit images that change like the wind. So much so that we now care more about how others view us and what they think of us than what God knows about us and has declared for our lives. Trying to impress people who may never be impressed. And the ones who maybe be impressed lack the proper ability to genuinely express it to you in a way that would be complimentary to you. Believe me when I say that being overly sensual and sensitive is a life full of consistent hurt and disappointment, if you haven't experienced it already. We must not allow our feelings to control us, lead us, or define us; we must fully grasp and embrace everything God has already predetermined us to be.

ADMIT IT

As we're on this journey together, I could only hope that your understanding is flowing like a river by now. Let's keep an uninterrupted flow then, shall we? I believe this is the perfect place to implement a verse of scripture that is vital for our growth and our freedom. Genesis 3:13 reads: *Then the Lord God said to the woman, "What is this you have done?" The woman said, "the serpent deceived me, and I ate."*

This very verse brings us to the place of a potential paradigm shift of our mindset like never before if we sincerely execute this. Beyond keying in on the fact that when God confronted Adam first about the incident, his answer was to blame the woman for giving him the fruit to eat. And of course, the blame game feels better and is easier to play. But the woman owned her stuff. The fact that she was aware that the enemy deceived her and admitted to it carried weight. This is the very place we must come to for ourselves as women.

I'm going to instruct you to carry this out in two parts. First, you must be able to own up to your own issues and hang ups. Be able to admit that "Yes, I have fallen prey to many if not all that was revealed in this chapter."

Admit, "Yes, this applies to me."

And you must be able to come to this realization without blaming someone else.

Admit, "I have allowed my issues, my personal feelings, emotions, and hang ups to shape my attitude and mindset. I have allowed those things to take over and define who I am and to dictate my course."

I'm sharing these as a roadmap on how you can go about this for yourself. I want you to take the time to do this exercise for yourself. Write down the things that you need to own up to and admit for yourself. Be brutally honest with yourself. Cut yourself no slack. Be very detailed. You know how we are as women. We can be extremely detailed, almost lawyer-like (lol). Whatever your hang ups are, put them on paper. Write them down. Read them out loud. Whether you battle with some form of insecurity, jealousy, envy, anger, being vindictive, having a nasty attitude, etc., whatever it is? Admit it. Admit how you have allowed these things to affect your life, attitude, mindset, decisions, relationships, communication, etc. Take this exercise seriously because there is freedom and liberty that will come from doing this.

Now, that part was personal, but let's travel a little bit deeper.

Don't do this part until you have fully done the first part I gave you. It is important to do it in the order I'm laying out here. For this second part of you admitting the truth to yourself, I understand that there are some occurrences that may have happened to you in life that were traumatic and completely out of your control. I mean serious stuff, whether you've been abused or violated in some way. They are to blame for any act committed against you; that was out of your control. Period! But! Who you have become is your responsibility. It *is* in your control. And if you feel you have somehow lost that control, then prepare to take it back! Admit, "I have allowed past situations, circumstances, dysfunctional relationships, and hurt to shape my mindset about myself."

Admit, "I have allowed life to put labels on me that are beneath the value the Lord has placed on me."

Admit, "I have allowed the world and people who do not know their own identity or value to diminish my perspective of myself."

Admit, "I've allowed Hollywood, television personalities, social media, broken people, and the like to give me a distorted image of myself and redefine me as a woman."

I'm giving you a template, but make it your own. When this is done right with much detail that you can go back and read for yourself, it will open your eyes and cause you to realize things and cause you to desire a real breakthrough to a better mindset. Woman, you must do this! Because there are avenues of success in various areas of your life waiting on you to show up!

QUEENDOM QUOTE

"The brave woman not only admits her faults but
works diligently to change for the better!"

NATASHA OQUENDO

LET'S PRAY...

Lord, You are El Roi, the God that sees me!

Nothing about my life is hidden from You!

I set my shortcomings, dysfunctions,

faults, and mistakes before You!

I admit them!

I confess them!

By the blood of Jesus cleanse

my heart, mind, and body!

Cause my attitude, mindset, and personality to line

up with the elevation You have ordained for me!

Grant me the power of emotional

control and stability!

Fill my heart with the braveness to

change for the better!

Lord, I thank You that every change

will yield powerful results!

In Jesus name!

Amen!

3RD KEY

BE DESPERATE
FOR FREEDOM!

THE RELEASE

THE REALITY

This is the time to do a life inventory check. Let's begin to look at where you are now, where you have been, and where you're trying to go as a woman. In this part of the journey, I will deal with a very delicate aspect of our lives. You may even say downright personal. But in doing so, I know this is needed for growth and overall breakthrough. The positions that I'm getting ready to address in this chapter we women have at some point found ourselves in whether it be past, present, or even the future. Please know that this manuscript is a safe zone designed to bring the understanding needed to break curses, negative mindsets, and overall negative life cycles. My suggestion is that you approach this area with an openness and hunger for freedom and a release from every entanglement.

As I take a sober look at us as women in our society, I have come to realize a very hard truth. Many of us struggle to find our self-worth from within. As a matter of fact, we constantly look to find validation through the acceptance and approval of men. This concept runs very deep. A great percentage of how confident we feel about ourselves and the way we look is dependent upon a man's perception of us. Think about it; no woman wants to be the categorized by a man as undesirable. So a lifestyle of countless time and effort is spent trying to remain desirable to the male counterpart. Many women do this by way of various surgeries to enhance their self-image to stay valid in a world that continues to change its view on what beauty really is. Whatever the popular thing that a man desires in a woman's appearance at the time becomes the woman's ultimate goal to become. If it's big breasts, big butts, full lips etc., then augmentation of the body becomes the norm. This trend has not only become popular but has more so become an epidemic of self-mutilation instead of improvement. Why? Because the standard of beauty is constantly changing to the point that nothing is never enough.

The very root of this mindset can be found in Genesis 3:16, which reads: To the woman he said, "I will make your pains in childbearing very severe, with painful labor you will give birth to children. Your desire will be for your husband, and he will rule over you."

Now this verse was the consequence for the woman after being deceived by the serpent in the Garden of Eden when she disobeyed God's instruction about eating the fruit from the tree of the knowledge of good and evil. I want to bring awareness to the part that says, "your desire will be for your husband, and he will rule over you." The lasting effects from this consequence, or curse for a better word, is ongoing. The desires for a husband, male affection, attention, and companionship are normal for a woman, right? The man in the position to rule over the woman is the normal way of operation, right? Well, to us today maybe so, but it was not God's original plan or intention. Remember, this was the consequence for the woman going against God's command. So, let's explore this, because the desire for a husband has not only become increasingly prevalent but it has escalated into a manifestation of desperation. It has ignited in most an unquenchable appetite to be loved and the unhealthy willingness to do anything for that love. And mind you, I am a firm believer that we still have not fully grasped the love concept. This desperation has become the ruling factor of the very life and existence of a woman. This thing goes beyond just a mere position of order in the land as the man being the head of the woman, but more so has spiraled into the man ruling every aspect of the woman until she doesn't have her own identity. How a woman feels about herself is predicated on how a man views her, feels about her, treats her, etc. This even controls how much confidence a woman will possess. If you find a woman who has low self-esteem and a lack of confidence, then it has most likely resulted from some form of rejection or mistreatment from a man in her life. Whether it was a father figure, husband, boyfriend, etc., the fact remains that most women base their worth and identity in the man they marry, date, or sleep with. In this society, the more men who desire you the more valuable you are. And women from all walks of life are fighting hard daily to stay in the contest.

AWW SILLY ME

As we go deeper into the consequences the Lord handed to the woman, it leads me into this concept found in 2 Timothy 3:1-7 (NIV):

> But mark this: There will be terrible times in the last days. ² People will be lovers of themselves, lovers of money, boastful, proud, abusive, disobedient to their parents, ungrateful, unholy, ³ without love, unforgiving, slanderous, without self-control, brutal, not lovers of the good, ⁴ treacherous, rash, conceited, lovers of pleasure rather than lovers of God—⁵ having a form of godliness but denying its power. Have nothing to do with such people.

> ⁶ They are the kind who worm their way into homes and gain control over gullible women, who are loaded down with sins and are swayed by all kinds of evil desires, ⁷ always learning but never able to come to a knowledge of the truth.

These verses are a visible depiction of what we can see taking place if our physical eyes are open, right? It gives us the vivid explanation of how people are truly operating in these last days. I am almost certain that we can relate to and confirm much of the text. So, the text is saying that men who love themselves more than God, or anybody else for that matter, will be very prevalent in the last days. It more specifically says that these are the kind of men who will find their way into the home/life of a silly/gullible woman. There are some key things I want to expound on to help us. In verse 6 of the passage, the term used to describe women is the word "silly" or "gullible." This term sounds offensive, right? Especially, when we don't understand the true message that is being conveyed to us. "Silly" means to exhibit or indicate a lack of common sense or good sound judgement. The word silly is used to convey that an activity or process has been engaged in to such a degree that the person is no longer capable of thinking or acting sensibly. Other words used to describe the word silly are weak minded, reckless, erratic, unstable, scatterbrained, flighty, immature, childish, irresponsible, thick headed, misguided, inappropriate, inadvisable, unreasonable, and gullible. Now the word silly can infiltrate many areas of our lives, but this is directive in nature. Remember, in verse 7 it said that we would be always learning but never able to come to a knowledge of the truth. I don't believe this had anything to do with our education or intelligence, for that matter, but more so our ability to discern the right man to let into our lives.

The word gullible means to be easily persuaded to believe something (credulous—to be easily deceived, having, or showing too great a readiness to believe things). Some synonyms are unsuspecting, unguarded, naïve, simple, green, ignorant, foolish, and silly. This led me to the word gullibility, which means a failure of social intelligence in which a person is easily tricked or manipulated into ill-advised course of action.

By sharing these words, I wanted to broaden our perception a bit because there is something much deeper that has happened to us. This is some of the aftermath from the effects of Eve's encounter with the serpent. Remember the serpent deceived the first woman in creation. And now here we are in the last days of the scripture in a full-fledged battle with the spirit of silliness, which really means a lack of accurate discernment and judgement when it comes to a man. When we as women choose to remain entangled (loaded down in sins, as the scripture put it), then we are prone to draw the type of men into our lives described in 2 Timothy 3:1-7. It becomes a way of life, almost like a revolving door, drawing this type of man in and out of our lives repeatedly and yielding the same negative results. And let me clarify, this concept applies whether you're saved or not saved, because I have seen many saved women who serve God and pray and speak in tongues—the whole nine yards—but when it comes to this area of discernment concerning a man, they remain gullible and entangled. How many of us can be completely honest right here and admit to falling into repeat situations with the wrong guys over and over? How many of us keep learning the same lessons from each situation but are still not able to acknowledge the truth of these repeat circumstances? It can be so crazy until you realize that you keep drawing the exact same type of guy but in a different body, with the same outcomes, leading to dysfunction and a trail of broken hearts and relationships. The truth is there are some spiritual entanglements, or should I say yokes, that must be broken and completely destroyed off of our lives as women.

Regardless of what you think you might want in a man, or whatever requirements you have listed that you want in a man, you will only draw what is attached to you spiritually. The scary part is, how many times will this happen before we honestly recognize the truth? Some of us are in relationships right now with people who our entanglements have drawn to us, and we wonder why marriages or relationships are loaded with chaos and heaviness. It is because the spirit of silliness and its lack of discernment established it. Desire turned to desperation has settled for it. Though your heart screams loudly for love, joy, and peace, your spirit has drawn turmoil and disappointment; always looking and blaming outside for the answers that can only truly be found within. Oh, I declare your release today!

THE STRANGE WOMAN

This part of the process leads me to a very popular story of when Jesus encounters a Samaritan woman at the well. It begins with him asking her for a drink of water. Mind you, it was strange for him to take the time to converse with this woman because the Jewish customs of that day deemed it unlawful. So, after she serves him the drink of water he asked for, Jesus goes into this elaborate explanation about water that he can supply her with so that she doesn't have to keep coming to the natural well to receive. Of course, he was speaking a parable to her about eternal life, but there were some key things that took place in this encounter. In John 4:15-19 (NIV), it states:

> *15 The woman said to him, "Sir, give me this water so that I won't get thirsty and have to keep coming here to draw water."*
>
> *16 He told her, "Go, call your husband and come back."*
>
> *17 "I have no husband," she replied.*
>
> *Jesus said to her, "You are right when you say you have no husband. 18 The fact is, you have had five husbands, and the man you now have is not your husband. What you have just said is quite true."*
>
> *19 "Sir," the woman said, "I can see that you are a prophet.*

First and foremost, I want to reiterate the fact that Jesus was offering this woman an alternative drink that had nothing to do with the natural realm because he knew her issue was spiritual. He knew that nothing in the natural realm could quench her desperation or fill the void she was experiencing. Now it is in verse 16 where things take a complete shift! He addresses the woman by what he sees spiritually over her life. He instructs her to go get her husband and come back! She replies that she does not have a husband, pretty much letting him know she is not legally married. Jesus in return lets her know that she has had five husbands and the man she was dealing with at that time was not her husband, either. So, spiritually she was clothed in the spirit of six men, and Jesus was prophetically able to see that covering her life.

Let me explain. You see, in biblical times they didn't just have a wedding ceremony to solidify marriage. You were considered husband and wife when you had sex. In the scriptures they would use the term "lay with." So, I called this a strange encounter because Jesus identified this woman by the strange spirits she was covered by. Her identity was disguised by the spirits of the six men whom she had slept with. Jesus had to address this strange woman's spirit on her life to help her move forward. I call her a strange woman because Jesus addressed her by the six husbands, he saw over her and not by her own identity. Though she appeared to him alone and unmarried according to the natural eye, there were six other spirits holding her identity captive. Spiritually, her personal identity was not able to be seen. This is what you call a strange woman. It has nothing to do with a physical appearance but more to do with a loss of identity. And many of us as women have lost who we really are in this same way.

Listen, spiritually the man has been given the ability to cover the woman, and spiritually the woman has been given the vulnerability to be covered. Sex is not only a physical pleasure but a spiritual act, that's why the Bible says the marriage bed is undefiled. We have made sex a casual thing, but it is really a sacred thing in the eyes of God. The Bible declares the two shall become one flesh. As a woman, when you open yourself up to become vulnerable to have sex with a man, his spirit becomes your covering. This is the reason why as a woman there is such a strong emotional attachment to who you have sex with. And when the emotional attachment is no longer there, it is because there have been multiple partners. Most of the men who will be attracted to your life, though different, will have that similarity of spirit about them. With this woman at the well there was something broken in her life; though she had been with various men there was still an unquenchable thirst in her that could not be satisfied with anything earthly. Whatever the desire turned to desperation was, it was carrying behind it a trail of broken relationships that caused her to completely lose her identity in the spirit world.

Yes, when we sleep with multiple men outside of marriage, we lose ourselves! Our true identity is stolen from us! We can be beautiful, smart, and even appear successful in the natural realm, but spiritually our true identity is lost. And listen, this cannot be ignored because I know of situations where women have gone into marriages with a strange spirit. Where the husband was attracted to the strange spirit, meaning the experiences the woman has had with other men. Her promiscuity, lustful nature, and the like is what drew him in the first place. When situations are like this, the relationship suffers because it lacks a development of true love. This was vitally important because Jesus dealt with it before the woman at the well could truly go on to be productive. He wanted to use her to bring people to him. Her strange spirit would have been a hindrance to the work, but later in the passage she was able to draw people to come and hear Jesus speak. This would not have been successful if she had not allowed him to deal with the strange spirit over her life first.

This is extremely important because the spirit of the strange woman is a direct enemy to any form of favor from God. Proverbs 2:16-19 (NIV) reads:

*16 Wisdom will save you also from the adulterous woman,
from the wayward woman with her seductive words,*

*17 who has left the partner of her youth and ignored the covenant
she made before God.[a]*

*18 Surely her house leads down to death and her paths to the
spirits of the dead.*

19 None who go to her return or attain the paths of life.

I have seen this spirit on a woman's life wreak havoc in the life of
a man. From negative effects on the man's health, business, finances,
etc. Anytime the enemy desires to destroy a man, especially if he is a
man of God, then all he does is send a woman with a strange spirit
to take him down. I've seen this spirit in operation; as soon as the
man gets with a woman who has a strange spirit everything starts
going downhill, even to the point of how he looks. Think about it,
the Bible says, "he who finds a wife, finds a good thing, and obtains
favor from the Lord" (Proverbs 18:22).

But the woman must be processed into the spirit of a wife first so
that the husband that God has ordained for her can find her.

THE CONCUBINE

As I approach this particular topic, I'm reminded of how blessed I was
when the Lord revealed this powerful understanding to me. I mean
this experience literally changed my life. When I rededicated my life
back to the Lord over twenty-two years ago, I came into the church
with my husband, who was my boyfriend at the time (we were what
they called "shacking" back then, lol). We were in a relationship, living
together, and having sex but not legally married. I gave my life back
to the Lord during an altar call one Sunday and my life has never
been the same since. I'm giving you the short form of my testimony
to get to the relevant part. The day I gave my life back to the Lord, I

almost immediately got convicted about my living situation. You see, this conviction took me on a journey with God that caused this revelation that I'm sharing with you to be something so real and tangible. I came home that same day and shared my conviction with my boyfriend and told him I could no longer continue to live in sexual sin. No one said anything to me at the church about fornication or shacking or anything. God strongly convicted me, and my eyes were wide open the day I renewed my salvation. Now, mind you we had been living together for a little over a year and had previously been talking about getting married.

The following week, he came to the church with me and rededicated his life back to the Lord, as well. At that point we knew that getting married was inevitable. He asked me to marry him, and we sat down together and decided on a wedding date nine months later. At that time, we were just going to go to the courthouse and have a simple ceremony. We decided to abstain from all sexual activity until after the wedding. I want you to know that those nine months were absolutely life-changing. The Holy Spirit led me to fast and pray during those nine months and also said that He would reveal and confirm that this was the husband he had for me. During this process, the Lord revealed that He was breaking the spirit of the concubine off my life. I had no clue what it meant but I began to search it out! The word "concubine" can be seen from two scenarios. The first as a woman who is a mistress to a man who has a wife. Mind you, this is recognized beneath the status of a wife. The next is a woman who has a sexual relationship with a man when they're not legally married. So, the second scenario applied to my life at that time and here I was, living with my boyfriend, performing all the duties of a wife, but spiritually not being recognized in the status of a wife. Whew!

As this was being revealed to me, I thought about past relationships, and once I realized that those past yokes could affect the marriage I was getting ready to enter, I began to do the work. We both did. As God guided me through this process of freeing me from every past entanglement and destroying those yokes, I began to truly see the value in myself and the man I was getting ready to marry. I paid attention to the fact that his navigation did not change because we were not entertaining sex. We communicated a whole lot. We set standards and boundaries concerning our marriage. We knew that adultery and abuse were what we called "deal breakers." We came to realize that many of our views and outlook on marriage were similar; that we both took the concept of marriage very seriously. We spent time bonding and enjoying each other's company, and this has carried on into our marriage to this very day.

We ended up experiencing so much favor from God that it was overwhelming. We went through six months of premarital counseling with our pastors, and they approved our marriage. We had a nice-sized wedding at the church. We were blessed with the invitations, photography, food, and decorations for the reception, and thousands in financial gifts! Remember, our humble plans were to go to the courthouse. We just wanted to make things right in the eyes of God, and God confirmed our union with His favor! As I thought about this process, I thought about how many of us women don't understand how the enemy tries to rob us of our status as a wife in the spirit world. The more we entertain these types of situations and relationships, the more we are diminishing our true rank in the spirit.

I have seen situations where women have been molded into being content as a married man's mistress and marriage would never be presented to them, even if the man left his wife. Literally, they would get married to a totally different woman than the mistress. And the mistress remained in her position as a mistress while he took on a new wife. I've also seen these situations show up in families as generational curses. Passed from great grandmother, to grandmother, to mother, to daughter, and so forth. From the stage of silliness to the spirit of the strange woman, to the concubine spirit, each phase must be addressed and spiritually broken off our lives.

And, may I add, the act of marriage after one has entertained these various phases of entanglements does not break the power of these spiritual bondages. I've seen people who think marriage is the answer for their lust, promiscuity, and various other sexual appetites, never realizing that it is only a cover up for a deeper spiritual problem that must be taken care of through spiritual means. Isaiah 58:6 says: "Is this not the kind of fasting I have chosen? To lose the bands of wickedness, to undo the heavy burdens, and to let the oppressed go free, and that you break every yoke."

Yes, you can go into a marriage or relationship with these yokes, but either the marriage will suffer or you will unknowingly become accommodated with carrying the yoke and heaviness. When these entanglements are still prevalent in your life, you not only risk drawing the wrong mate, but those various entanglements will fight against your mate spiritually. The dysfunctional experiences and mannerisms developed in those past relationships and encounters will show up in your present marriage or relationship as issues. Spiritually, your mind will always revert to those past experiences to interact with the present person you're dealing with, thereby not giving them a fresh start or a fighting chance. All the issues from those past situations will show up and literally act themselves out. Like I said, it's spiritual!

QUEENDOM QUOTE

"A bold woman who realizes her worth will cut off every entanglement that has sold her short and reclaim her full value with interest!"

NATASHA OQUENDO

LET'S PRAY...

Lord, You are a mighty Deliverer!

By the blood of Jesus I completely denounce

every soul tie that has entangled my life!

Forgive me for not knowing my worth and being

reckless with the high value you have placed on

me! Remove every strange spirit that

covers my true identity!

Wash me from every wifely duty I've performed

for men who were not the husband You

designated for me!

Cleanse me from all the damage my past

and present encounters have caused!

Renew my life and spirit!

Grant me wisdom from above, pure discernment,

and sound judgement from this day forth!

In Jesus mighty name!

Amen!

4TH KEY

BE CONSUMED
WITH
DETERMINATION!

THE WHOLE WOMAN

WILL YOU?

In some form or fashion, life has happened to us all! But we can come to a defining moment within our life experience where we must answer a very vital question: "Will you be made whole?"

This question derives from the encounter Jesus has with a man near the pool of Bethesda. John 5:1-9 key verse 6 (KJV) reads:

> *After this there was a feast of the Jews; and Jesus went up to Jerusalem.* *²Now there is at Jerusalem by the sheep market a pool, which is called in the Hebrew tongue Bethesda, having five porches.* *³In these lay a great multitude of impotent folk, of blind, halt, withered, waiting for the moving of the water.* *⁴For an angel went down at a certain season into the pool and troubled the water: whosoever then first after the troubling of the water stepped in was made whole of whatsoever disease he had.* *⁵And a certain man was there, which had an infirmity thirty and eight years.* *⁶When Jesus saw him lie, and knew that he had been now a long time in that case, he saith unto him, Will thou be made whole?* *⁷The impotent man answered him, Sir, I have no man, when the water is troubled, to put me into the pool: but while I am coming, another steps down before me.* *⁸Jesus saith unto him, Rise, take up thy bed, and walk.* *⁹And immediately the man was made whole, and took up his bed, and walked: and on the same day was the sabbath.*

Now there are a few things that I must unpack from this passage. First, let's look at the man's response when Jesus asks him the question "Will you be made whole?"

The man brings attention to two reasons as to why he has not gotten into the pool to be healed. He says, there is no man to put him into the pool and that when he comes to get in someone else steps into the pool before him. So, he has the mindset that he has not gotten his healing because an outside source has not helped him. He has focused on the fact that someone else stepped into the pool ahead of him while he was coming. While these instances were his reality, they were not the truth! Think about it, he was stuck and stagnated in his condition, and he blamed others for him not being able to get to the place of healing. His mindset reminds me of many of us and how we put the focus of our problems on outside sources.

How many times have we highlighted who hasn't done things to help us? Or become a broken record about all the negative things others have done to us, not realizing that because we have chosen to focus on these things is part of the real reason, and we have become stuck and stagnated from moving forward in life? For some reason, there is comfort in putting the blame on others when we are stuck in life, situations, circumstances, or problems we're facing. Notice when Jesus responds to the man, he never addresses any of the excuses the man has made as to why he has not gotten into the pool to be healed, but commands him to Rise, to take up his bed, and to walk! Those instructions were given directly to the man.

Jesus shifted the focus back to the man himself and what he had to do to be healed. This is what we must do to experience our healing and begin our journey to being made whole. We must rise up from all our excuses and take responsibility for our personal well-being. We must take back our power to decide to rise from whatever our conditions may be.

Now, let me rephrase the question, "Is it your will to be made whole?"

Let's look at the word "will." Will means the faculty by which a person decides on and initiates action. In other words, based on this definition, let me ask it like this: How long has it taken you to make the solid decision and initiate the action it's going to take for you to be made whole? Because some synonyms for the word will are decision, determination, willpower, drive tenacity, dedication, and singlemindedness. The decision, determination, and willpower to be made whole cannot come from outside sources; it must come from within you. This man's healing was not held up because no one would put him into the pool, or the fact that people beat him getting into the pool. The problem was his own WILL to be made whole! For thirty-eight long years he didn't have enough drive, determination, or willpower to be healed. Think about it, there were multitudes of people around that pool waiting for the moving of the water to get in! Just like there are multitudes of us out here now waiting on the season for God to move and heal our conditions and situations to make us whole. But God is looking for us to single-mindedly decide to be made whole. Who has the drive, dedication, tenacity, determination, and willpower to believe and take action? How long have you been in your situation or condition? Are you tired enough of your condition that when Jesus shows up, you will obey His words and make the moves necessary for change? Because it's going to take your full participation!

Now, I noticed in the passage that once the man decided to obey what Jesus told him to do, which was to "Rise, take up your bed and walk!" the man did not have to wait for the angel to trouble any water or beat anybody else getting into a pool. When his will decided, he was no longer bound to the traditional way of the pool. His healing came immediately! No more excuses! No more waiting! You better catch this one in the Spirit. WILL You?

WHY TOUCH?

Now that we have established that it's a yes to being made whole, let us continue in our pursuit, shall we? Let's visit Matthew 9:20-22: *And behold a woman which was diseased with an issue of blood twelve years, came behind him and touched the hem of his garment: For she said within herself, If I may but touch his garment, I shall be made whole. But Jesus turned about, and when he saw her, he said Daughter be of good comfort, thy faith have made thee whole. And the woman was made whole that very hour.*

I want to say that in this woman's pursuit to touch the hem of Jesus' garment there was a crowd of people who were touching Jesus and bumping into him as he was passing through this place. But there was something about this woman and her pursuit of him that could not be ignored or go unnoticed. Her pursuit caused her to experience an actual manifestation of his power. There was something about her that caused Jesus to respond to this woman and leave her whole. As I pondered this, the Lord reminded me of my own personal pursuit of him. In this he revealed a powerful answer that I must share with you. The thing that made her stand out and set her apart from many others in this scenario was her reason for touching him. Why did she believe she only needed to touch him? Why didn't she want him to lay hands on her like most? What was her true motive for wanting to touch Jesus? This is where the real answer lies to how she received the release of power to be made whole.

Think about it, she had been in that battle with her issue for twelve long years. She touched him because she knew she had an issue. Her issue was her reason. It was her issue that drove her to pursue him sincerely. She legitimately acknowledged that she had this issue and believed that only touching his clothes could resolve it. Just like this woman, I came into my salvation relentlessly, pursuing

Jesus to touch him through prayer because I knew I had issues. My issues were the motive that drove me to touch his presence. Like the woman with the issue of blood, his power was released into my life to make me whole. The reason was not to pursue him to get his power to become powerful. Not to seek him for riches. Not for a prominent title. Not to use my talent and have it make room for me. Not to activate some supernatural gifting to make me feel relevant and compensate for insecurities. Not to preach, teach, prophesy, or hold a microphone. No, not an ulterior motive whatsoever, but simply and honestly acknowledging the fact that I had issues within myself that could only be healed if I touched him.

You see, it is the personal issues within that should ignite the sincere pursuit to rightfully touch him. She didn't say, "If I touch Jesus, I can become somebody important that everybody will respect."

She didn't say, "If I touch him, I can gain some power or gift that will bring me attention."

Not, "If I touch him, I can do like Jesus and heal people or cast out devils."

No, it was her issues that made her pursuit pure and her wholeness inevitable. Our motives and intentions to touch Jesus must come from a pure place if we're going to be made whole. We must be real with him about our issues if we're going to experience real and lasting results. I have seen the disappointment of trying to touch him without acknowledging the issues. When people try to touch him with impure motives and preconceived agendas, they are left without his power and remain with their same issues. Whew!

Let's reevaluate and revisit our reason for wanting to touch him. Let our real issues drive us to the place to truly touch him and be made whole. Because it is our reason for touching him that will determine our outcome.

THE DETERMINATION

As I approach this point, I want to share it from Mark's perspective of the woman with the issue of blood. Mark 5:25-28 (NIV) reads:

> [25] *And a woman was there who had been subject to bleeding for twelve years.* [26] *She had suffered a great deal under the care of many doctors and had spent all she had, yet instead of getting better she grew worse.* [27] *When she heard about Jesus, she came up behind him in the crowd and touched his cloak,* [28] *because she thought, "If I just touch his clothes, I will be healed."*

So not only had this woman established that her issue was her reason for touching Jesus, but Mark's account of this story reveals yet another factor. Verse 26 goes a step further and says she suffered a great deal under the care of many doctors. So, she's seeing various doctors and none of them can resolve her issue. Then it says she spent all that she had. Now we all know that medical bills can be a monster. This woman literally exhausted her resources trying to get relief from her issue and the text says she got worse. This seems to be a very familiar pattern, because most things tend to get worse before better shows up.

This reminds me of an experience I had back in 2005. I was dealing with some severe abdominal pains that landed me in the hospital, where they diagnosed me with an ovarian cyst. I remember they gave me an ultrasound picture of the cyst and everything. I went back to my doctor's appointment and the diagnosis got worse. They told me it was a tumor the size of a golf ball. I left that place with an assignment to fast, pray, and pursue the presence and word of God like never before! I will never forget that the Lord spoke to me in my prayer closet at 3 a.m., the morning of my next appointment, and said he was going to heal me divinely. I believed the word of the

Lord! I went to my appointment, only for them to refuse to see me because I did not have insurance. That literally felt like a blow to my stomach! I remember that moment feeling like all the wind got knocked out of me! Angry and disappointed I went to my car, and I heard the Lord say, "Didn't I say I was going to heal you divinely?"

It was at that moment I realized that my circumstances had me in a position that only the Lord could help me out of! I was provoked and determined to touch him, much like the woman with the issue of blood. I continued to fast, pray, sow seeds, and get in his presence, declaring his word over my life. Mind you, the painful episodes I was having were real. Not only that, but attacks were coming in other areas of my life at the same time. Yes, everything seemingly got worse before my better showed up. The Holy Spirit prompted me to pray, so I crawled into my prayer closet, wracked with pain, at about 3 a.m. one morning, wrapped in my prayer blanket groaning and rocking back and forth. Then suddenly, I felt it break! I felt the spirit of infirmity lift! The pain immediately ceased! Sweat poured from me like a faucet of running water. My prayer blanket was completely drenched! Then I heard the Lord say, "You are healed!"

That spirit was broken, and I knew it. About seven months later I was finally able to afford some insurance and went to get a checkup. I told the doctor about the previous diagnosis I had received, and they ran all the necessary tests and there was no sign of ovarian cysts or tumors! I received a clean bill of health and confirmation that God had done just what he said, healed me!

I shared my testimony to confirm the story of the woman with the issue of blood. The fact that my issue gave me the drive and desperation I needed to genuinely touch Jesus. And listen, the issue can be anything. From health issues, mental issues, emotional issues, personality issues, character issues, attitude issues, and the like. All things personal; especially all things within. God will allow these things so that you can pursue and genuinely acknowledge Him.

Your unresolved issue has the power to provoke you to pursue Jesus to a place to touch him for real. The fact that you are reading this book lets me know that you are not just here by happenstance. No! Something has provoked you to this place! To this encounter! This is your time and your opportunity to be provoked to touch him! Sincerely and earnestly pursue to touch him until he loses power on your behalf to make you whole!

WHAT DO YOU BELIEVE?

It is what you believe that has the power to determine your results. Luke 8:48 (KJV) reads: *And he said unto her "Daughter, be of good comfort: thy faith hath made thee whole, go in peace."*

Remember, this woman said within herself that if she could just touch Jesus' clothes that she would be made whole. She truly believed this from within herself. This is the reason that we must deal with the issues within us first because they can block us from believing to the point of not receiving results! She believed, pursued, and her faith in action made her whole. Now, let me clarify, her faith was not her ability to touch Jesus, but more so in His ability to heal and make her whole. This is major because most times we focus on our ability to do something.

Let's just be honest; the woman did not know beyond a shadow of a doubt that she would physically be able to actually touch Jesus. She was not focused on her ability to press through the crowd that surrounded him. I'm sure her issue with blood caused her to experience some level of weakness. My point is that her physical strength and abilities were limited. This is why I asked the question, "What do you believe?" Because just believing in her own personal strength and ability was not enough to get the powerful results she experienced.

She knew from experience that the power to make her whole was not found in the doctors or anything else. She was convinced that the resolution for her issue was found in him. Her issue was blood related, but the issue can be whatever issue happening within you that plagues your life. I tend to believe that it was the woman's belief in the ability of Jesus that gave her the strength to press her way through the crowd and touch his clothes.

Think about it, she believed so intensely that her faith told her he was so powerful that his mere clothes carried the power to heal her! And Jesus said her faith is what made her whole. When was the last time you believed in Jesus to this degree with your issue? The word "issue" means any personal problem or difficulty. There is no issue too hard or too personal for him to resolve. Feelings of loneliness, harboring bitterness, unforgiveness, self-esteem issues, insecurities, jealousy, envy, covetousness, mental issues, desperation, etc. The list can go on for miles. Regardless of what it may be, you must truly believe that your wholeness and healing is found in touching him. Not a man, not a marriage, not a relationship, not friends, not drugs, alcohol, or sex, etc. No! Not in any other thing that can be used to temporarily medicate your issue. None of those things yield a lasting resolution to your problems. But Jesus contains the ultimate power to heal and make you whole. Be sincere, believe, and pursue.

BE MADE WHOLE

All this talk about being made whole has led us to another very important question: Do we really understand what it means to "Be made whole?"

Often when it's mentioned, it refers to some form of healing or being delivered from some situation, circumstance, or people that we feel have left us hurt and broken. We even think of it from the aspect of breaking free from relationships and positions that didn't allow us the freedom to be or express ourselves in our entirety. Now, don't get me wrong, all of these are wonderful, but not the true meaning of being made whole. I believe these are some of the results that could manifest from being made whole, but not the actual wholeness itself. These and much more are outward manifestations of something that has taken place on a much deeper level.

Let's look at the meaning of the word "whole." Whole means the full quantity, amount, extent, number, etc., without exception; entire, full, or total. To contain all the elements that properly belong; complete. To be undivided; in one piece. A thing complete in itself or having all its parts or elements. The best example of this definition is found in the perfect alignment of the Father, the Son, and the Holy Spirit!

1 John 5:7 reads: *For there are three that bear record in heaven, the Father, the Word, and the Holy Spirit: and these three are one. Though they exist in three parts, they function in perfect alignment and agreement as one.*

The Bible also states that we are made in the image and likeness of God. He created us as three-part beings as well. We as human beings are made up of spirit, soul, and body. The spirit is our innermost part. It is the part of us that is God-conscious. It is the place where we can connect and communicate with God. Next is the soul, consisting of the mind which includes the conscience, the will, and the emotions. Then, there's the body, which is the physical exterior of a person. It is the part of man that can be seen. So, there are the three parts of God as the Father, the Son Jesus—also known as the Word—and the Holy Spirit. Then there is the three parts to our human existence as the spirit, the soul, and the body.

Let's line them up. God connects with our spirit. Jesus connects with our soul. The Holy Spirit connects with our body. Now, to say we are made whole is to say that our spirit, soul, and body are in perfect alignment and agreement with one another. All three must believe the same thing. They all must function in oneness based on the belief. Most times we are not whole because our spirit, which is God-conscious, knows a truth, but our soul will struggle to agree and align with that truth.

Our soul is what gives our body the power to carry out what we believe. Remember, the soul contains our will, and our will is where we decide on things and initiate actions. When our soul decides on something, it gives our body the willpower, determination, drive, tenacity, and dedication necessary to carry out the action. When our spirit, soul, and body are not in agreement then we become stuck and stagnated in life. Yes, we are literally unable to move forward productively in life.

We saw this in operation with the man near the pool of Bethesda. He was stuck in that same position for thirty-eight years waiting for the moving of the water. I believe Jesus showed up and spoke directly to his soul, and his soul agreed when Jesus said, "Rise, take up your bed and walk!" His body was able to align itself and he was thereby able to produce movement.

You see, I don't believe we're waiting on God to do anything. I believe He has already done everything. We are in waiting because it takes time for our soul to believe and agree and then initiate our body to action with what God has said concerning us. We get no manifestation because we are out of alignment. When you're in alignment, you're in a position of easy agreement. Things are lined up and put in order! Alignment is when our thoughts, life choices, and actions line up with our belief system.

Amos 3:3 says: *Can two walk together except they be agreed?*

Notice that the word agree is directly connected to walking, which is a physical act of movement. This concept not only applies to us being whole but also to various areas of our lives, for that matter! It begins with us as an individual first, but then it flows into our households because the Bible says in Matthew 12:25 that a house divided shall not stand.

This also spirals into our relationships, businesses, ministries, etc. All these areas of our lives are affected when our spirit, soul, and body are out of alignment, agreement, and oneness. *It is the spirit that is willing, but it is the flesh that is weak* (Matthew 26:41).

I want to also reiterate the fact that both the man near the pool of Bethesda and the woman with the issue of blood were both weak in their physical bodies due to their conditions, but when their souls came into agreement with their spirit while they were in the presence of Jesus, their physical bodies were able to receive the willpower and determination to produce movement that was otherwise not humanly possible.

QUEENDOM QUOTE

"The woman who has decided that wholeness is her portion will pursue it with everything she's got and settle for nothing less than victory!"

NATASHA OQUENDO

LET'S PRAY...

Lord You are God the Father, God the Son,

and God the Holy Spirit!

These three are one!

I believe that my wholeness can only be found in

You! Father, bring my spirit, soul, and body into

alignment and agreement, as You are!

Mend the areas where I am broken!

You are Jehovah Rapha!

The God who heals me!

Heal my entire life from the inside out!

I decree, I have been supernaturally graced to

pursue You until I am made whole!

Nothing lacking and nothing missing!

With great faith, determination, and all my issues

I touch the hem of Your garment!

You ask me will I be made whole?

I cast down every excuse!

My answer is yes! I receive it now!

In Jesus name! Amen!

5TH KEY

RESPECT
THE
ORDER

ALL THINGS DAUGHTER

THE TITLE

There are so many discrepancies that surround this title "daughter," so I want to approach it from a position of clarity. There are various phrases that are used such as "daughter in the faith," "Spiritual daughter," or "daughter in the Spirit." I have come to recognize the genuineness and the corruption of its usage. My hope is that this is shared in such a way that it ignites a clear and healthy perception.

When we look at the word "daughter" it means a girl or a woman's offspring in relation to either or both of her parents. It is a woman considered in relation to her native country or area. A daughter is also a woman considered as the product of a particular person, influence, or environment. From these meanings, we get the daughter being birthed from her original parents. Next is a daughter of her native place of birth and location. Then, there is a daughter who is a byproduct of a person or environment that has influenced, nurtured, or cultivated them in some capacity. So, you're not only considered the daughter of your natural birth parents, but also the country, city, and state you're born in. You are also considered a daughter of the environment you've been subjected to, and by what has influenced your life, belief system, and decisions. From a biological standpoint, the word daughter means to originate through replication. To replicate is to make an exact copy of, to reproduce, or duplicate. So, you literally can become a replica or duplicate of an individual's faith, belief system, and way of life. By looking at this, we can easily come to realize that the concept of being a daughter in the natural and in the spiritual are pretty much the same.

Just as you're born into this natural world as a daughter, you're born into the spiritual world as a daughter. You are a daughter before you become a woman. Likewise, you are a daughter in the faith or spiritual daughter before you become a woman of God. And think about it, we go through an entire process to evolve from a daughter into a woman. That journey consists of a lot of being nurtured, guided, instructed, learning, growing, and developing; being equipped and prepared for life and womanhood.

This process is very similar in the spiritual sense, but the only difference is that you can be a grown woman in the natural and still must humble yourself to be a daughter again to be processed spiritually. And what must be realized is that the title of daughter is a very important title that stays with us. Yes, once you are a daughter you will always be considered the daughter of someone, someplace, and something.

IN THE FAITH

I want to investigate this title of "daughter" as it appears in an encounter that Jesus had with the woman with an issue of blood in Matthew 9:22 (KJV) that reads: *But Jesus turned him about, and when he saw her, he said, Daughter, be of good comfort, thy faith has made thee whole. And the woman was made whole from that hour.*

The woman presses her way through a crowd and succeeds in touching the hem of his clothes, power leaves him, enters her life, and makes her whole. Immediately after this takes place, he addresses her as the title of Daughter and says that it was her faith that made her whole. And because of this, her life took a major shift from being just a mere woman to the title of Daughter.

When we look at the word "faith," it means complete trust or confidence in someone or something. It is a strong belief in God or the doctrines of religion based on spiritual comprehension rather than proof. It is a strongly held system of religious beliefs and theories. Think about this for a minute, the Bible says that faith comes by hearing the Word of God (Romans 10:17). And Jesus Himself is the Word in flesh form. This woman heard that Jesus (the Word) was coming, and she strongly believed that when she touched his hem that she would be made whole. So, her confident belief in Jesus (the Word) and her willingness to put in the work to touch his hem is what qualified her to become a "Daughter in the Faith." Her belief and work in action together enabled her to receive the manifestation of her faith. Yes, she had to put some work into what she believed. The Bible says, *"faith without works is dead"* (James 2:20).

In essence, she became a byproduct of the person Jesus, and the environment of faith he represented influenced her. So yes, her belief in the Word is what made her whole. In this life, you can have faith and belief in anything. For this writing, I am using the example of faith and belief in God, Jesus Christ, and the Holy Spirit because this is my personal faith and belief system.

If you have faith, where did it come from? What did you hear? Who did you hear it from? Who influenced you to believe? In what place and environment was your faith developed and cultivated? The faith that you profess, how does it impact your decisions and the way you live your life? These and many other questions are worth pondering, but the point is to determine the origin of your belief; the who, what, where, when, why, and how you were birthed into your faith and belief system is vital.

Ruth is a perfect example of knowing where her faith originated and choosing to stick with it. Ruth 1:8-18 (NIV) reads:

⁸ Then Naomi said to her two daughters-in-law, "Go back, each of you, to your mother's home. May the Lord show you kindness, as you have shown kindness to your dead husbands and to me. ⁹ May the Lord grant that each of you will find rest in the home of another husband." Then she kissed them goodbye, and they wept aloud ¹⁰ and said to her, "We will go back with you to your people." ¹¹ But Naomi said, "Return home, my daughters. Why would you come with me? Am I going to have any more sons, who could become your husbands? ¹² Return home, my daughters; I am too old to have another husband. Even if I thought there was still hope for me—even if I had a husband tonight and then gave birth to sons— ¹³ would you wait until they grew up? Would you remain unmarried for them? No, my daughters. It is more bitter for me than for you because the Lord's hand has turned against me!" ¹⁴ At this they wept aloud again. Then Orpah kissed her mother-in-law goodbye, but Ruth clung to her. ¹⁵ "Look," said Naomi, "your sister-in-law is going back to her people and her gods. Go back with her." ¹⁶ But Ruth replied, "Don't urge me to leave you or to turn back from you. Where you go I will go, and where you stay I will stay. Your people will be my people and your God my God. ¹⁷ Where you die I will die, and there I will be buried. May the Lord deal with me, be it ever so severely, if even death separates you and me." ¹⁸ When Naomi realized that Ruth was determined to go with her, she stopped urging her.

This was powerful! Here was Naomi, the mother-in-law of Orpah and Ruth, who lost her husband and two sons who were married to these two women. Naomi was a woman of God who was experiencing a tremendous tragedy because of the death of her husband and two sons at the same time. In this, Orpah and Ruth are grieving the death of their husbands. Naomi pleads with them to go back to Moab where they are from in hopes of finding new husbands there. Orpah goes back to her home of Moab, but Ruth does not. There was a different faith and belief system in Moab because they worshipped a different god. For Ruth it was not just about her marriage or being able to remarry. She was planted in the faith and the God that Naomi lived her life for. Ruth chose God over having a new husband! She chose the best part. Ruth was no longer just a natural daughter-in-law, but she became Naomi's daughter in the faith! The origin of her faith in the True and Living God was established, and she decided to hold on to that faith even amid a painful loss! She stayed with Naomi because of her God!

IN THE SPIRIT

Just as we are born into this natural realm as a son or daughter, we must also experience being reborn as a spiritual son or daughter. To clarify this concept let's take a look at the conversation between Jesus and Nicodemus. John 3:1-7 says:

> *3 There was a man of the Pharisees named Nicodemus, a ruler of the Jews. 2 This man came to Jesus by night and said to Him, "Rabbi, we know that You are a teacher from God; for no one can do these signs that You do unless God is with him." 3 Jesus answered and said to him, "Most assuredly, I say to you, unless one is born again, he cannot see the kingdom of God." 4 Nicodemus said to Him, "How can a man be born when he is old? Can he enter a second time into his mother's womb and be born?" 5 Jesus answered, "Most assuredly, I say to you, unless one is born of water and the Spirit, he cannot enter the kingdom of God. 6 That which is born of the flesh is flesh, and that which is born of the Spirit is spirit. 7 You should not be surprised that I said to you, 'You must be born again.'*

In this passage, Jesus has made a distinction between being born in the natural and being born in the Spirit. Nicodemus was a grown man and could not return to his mother's womb, but he could experience being born again in the Spirit.

Nicodemus acknowledged that Jesus was a teacher of Israel. For this reason, the teaching influenced him enough to meet with Jesus and have that conversation. So, Nicodemus could have experienced a rebirth in the Spirit by becoming a byproduct of Jesus, influenced through his teachings, and the environment of faith that he created. In this same way, you can be birthed spiritually by the spirit of a leader who has submitted to, obeys, and operates under the power and manifestation of the Holy Spirit. It is their level of influence that impacts your life and belief system. In this way, you become a son or daughter of that belief system and way of life.

So, let's look into this. How do we become a "Spiritual daughter?" First, it takes a man or woman of God who believes in God the Father, the Son Jesus, and the Holy Spirit. They must be saved for real, baptized in the Holy Spirit, anointed by God with the assignment to be a leader to God's people, and processed to the point that God has authorized them to operate and function as a leader in that time. Now, I could really say a lot more about this because there are many men and women of God during this time who are under-processed but are still leading. And for this reason, many people are not being birthed correctly in the fullness of real, legitimate faith. At any rate, the man or woman of God must feed you the Word of God. Next, you must believe in the teaching to the capacity that it influences what you believe in, your mindset, your way of thinking, and ultimately your way of living your life! In this way, you are becoming a duplicate of what you believe. The goal of this process is to get enough of God's Word sown into your heart that it transforms your mind and sets you in a position to become a candidate to receive the baptism of the Holy Spirit.

Remember what Jesus told Nicodemus in John 3:5, Jesus answered, "I tell you the truth, No one can enter the kingdom of God unless he is born of water and the Spirit."

To be born of water is to be baptized with the teaching of God's Word that brings us to the place of repenting and turning away from sin. It's like listening to the Word of God until it reveals that our mind and body are filthy; needing a cleansing, detox, and bath. So, to be born of this water means we have developed the natural ability to receive the teaching of God's Word and apply it to areas of sin in our lives and allow it to cleanse and wash those sins from us. This means we have come to understand the Word's job in our lives, and we are not offended by it revealing our sin or the process it takes us through to get us clean.

Born of water means I'm suited and trained by this process and understand its task, which is to cleanse me from my sins and make me pleasing to God. This is an ongoing process that prepares you for the place to be "born of the Spirit." To be born of the Spirit, you must be baptized with teaching about the Holy Spirit by a leader who has been filled with the Holy Spirit. Yes, that individual must have the Holy Spirit. In this case, a person cannot impart what they don't have. And I will say this with full assurance that not everyone who claims to have the Holy Spirit actually does.

Let me take the time here to expound. Jesus gave a mandate to the leaders he placed in position in Matthew 28:18-20:

> *[18] Then Jesus came to them and said, "All authority in heaven and on earth has been given to me. [19] Therefore go and make disciples of all nations, baptizing them in the name of the Father and of the Son and of the Holy Spirit, [20] and teaching them to obey everything I have commanded you. And surely, I am with you always, to the very end of the age."*

In verse 19, Jesus tells his disciples/leaders to baptize those who will follow them in the name of the Father, and of the Son, and of the Holy Spirit. To be baptized in the name of the Father is teaching about God to the extent that you believe there is one God who exists. James 2:19 (NLT) says, *"You say you have faith, for you believe that there is one God, Good for you! Even the demons believe this, and they tremble in terror."*

The next step is to be baptized in the name of the Son. This is to be taught to believe in the teachings about Jesus. I want to share this biblical demonstration of the three baptisms from when Paul met Jesus on the road to Damascus (Acts chapter 9). At that time he was known as Saul, and I believe he was baptized in the teaching about God the Father because he believed that there was one God and that He did exist. But Paul was incomplete in his learning because he was killing people that belonged to God. On his way to Damascus, he had an encounter with the Lord that caused him to fall off his horse and be blinded. The Lord spoke to Paul and asked him why was he persecuting him? Think about it, because Paul only had the first baptism, he thought he was serving God but was persecuting Him by mistreating His saints. This happened because Paul was incomplete in his process. He only had the first baptism. In that encounter, Paul asks, "Who are you, Lord?"

Then the Lord answers, "I am Jesus."

So here we see the second baptism in operation with Paul encountering the presence of Jesus. Now after he encounters Jesus, he is still left blinded. He went to Damascus and waited three days for an anointed man of God who was filled with the Holy Spirit named Ananias, who laid hands on him and baptized him in the Holy Spirit. Once Paul received the Holy Spirit, that's when he received his sight. So you see, this scenario shows the three baptisms in operation. You can also see why the complete process of being baptized is necessary.

So, I go back to this about the spiritual parent/leader and why it is an absolute requirement that they have the Holy Spirit. They should be complete in all three baptisms if they're going to lead you through this process. And I mean consistently living in those baptisms for a substantial amount of time. This is the proper way that God has intended.

But what has happened is many teach others God's Word without the Holy Spirit? This means they teach from an incomplete place about God. They are teaching from their own human spirit and intellect. When this happens, the people who are fed and nurtured under that individual become a copy, replica, or duplicate of that person's human spirit. They take on the person's way of thinking and certain aspects of the person's nature, but not a clear pathway out of a life of sin or the development of a solid relationship with God.

Now, this can be a two-way street. Not only should the leader be held accountable, but us as followers are accountable, as well. This process can also go awry if a person filled with the Holy Spirit tries to teach and pour into someone who is resisting the truth of God's Word that brings one to a place of repentance from sin. When the person rejects the Holy Spirit through the individual they are being fed from, then they risk only taking on the outward appearance of the individual; meaning they may mimic or copy the person, but they don't truly receive the spiritual impartation from the person. They don't partake from that leader's level of faith. They risk learning only a form of godly outward appearance but have no real power against sin and the enemy. So yes, you can become a spiritual daughter of that leader who is feeding and influencing your life. This is possible whether the leader has the Holy Spirit or not. But the proper way God intended is to be birthed into a spiritual daughter by way of a leader filled with the Holy Spirit. This is a beautiful connection when it is true, because this is when the concept "know no man by the flesh" becomes priceless! The spiritual daughter can be trusted to join forces with their spiritual parents/leaders in bringing God's purpose and assignment to pass.

SPIRITUAL CONNECTIONS

As the term "spiritual parents" has become more and more popular, I want to try my best to help bring a greater understanding to this somewhat controversial and misunderstood topic. When we look at the word "parent," it means a mother or father. Parents are the source, origin, or cause of your existence. They can procreate and give birth to you. Mothers and fathers exercise paternal care over people; by definition they are protectors and providers. Parents not only tend to you but nurture and raise you.

Now, let's add the spiritual to this. When we're dealing with the spiritual side of things, it pertains to the realm of spirits in relation to the characteristics of the church, religion, or sacred things. It is the sphere of the intangible, such as the spirit and soul. The spiritual connection or relationship is more so based on communication between the souls and minds of the people involved. The spiritual is how we relate to, connect, and communicate with God. So spiritual parents are those who have been empowered by God to properly birth you in the Holy Spirit. God has caused them to be a source of you entering spiritual existence and connection with Him.

As I say this, I want to express a truth here. You do not have many spiritual parents in your life. You may have various leaders and mentors that you choose to follow in various areas for multiple reasons, but as for spiritual parents this is not the case. 1 Corinthians 4:14-16 (NKJV) reads: *14 I do not write these things to shame you, but as my beloved children I warn you. 15 For though you might have ten thousand instructors in Christ, yet you do not have many fathers;*

for in Christ Jesus, I have begotten you through the gospel. ¹⁶ Therefore
I urge you, imitate me.

A spiritual parent can have the capacity to birth you in the gospel
and continue to lead you as they follow Christ. They will provide
you with God's word with demonstration and understanding of the
spiritual lifestyle. They provide a protective covering over your life
by the authority God has given them: living holy, prayer, instruction,
correction, etc. Spiritual parents can birth you and lead you, but not
every leader is a spiritual parent. Your spiritual parents are going to
be the individuals who baptize you in the Holy Spirit and introduce
you to the lifestyle of the Spirit! It doesn't matter what leaders you
may be intrigued by and may follow whether via social media or
visiting other ministries. They can instruct you and even give you
guidance of all sorts, but they cannot give birth to you spiritually if
God has not ordained them to be able to procreate spiritually where
you're concerned.

Now, some spiritual parents, depending upon their level of spiritual endowment, may be able to birth you into the fundamentals of
being baptized in the Holy Spirit but cannot tend to, nurture, and
raise you spiritually. This is especially possible when spiritual parents
lack the understanding of their true role and how to execute their
assignment in your life. The best way I can describe it is when natural
parents get pregnant and have children too soon. This can happen in
the spiritual realm, as well. There are spiritual parents who started
ministries too soon and have given birth to spiritual children who
had to either go to another set of spiritual adoptive parents to finish
their process or try to raise themselves through the rest of the process.

Regardless of your situation, there are not many spiritual fathers
and mothers. You have the original spiritual parents that God has
ordained to truly birth you into genuine salvation. If those spiritual
parents are not the ones to spiritually cover you until you process to
the place of receiving the baptism of the Holy Spirit, then God will

enable spiritual adoptive parents to come into play. Thank God for those who may have contributed to your spiritual growth in whatever capacity, but they are not considered spiritual parents. They are considered instructors, mentors, or some form of leader.

Let's look into the role of the spiritual parent. Hebrews 13:17 (NLT) says:

> *Obey your [spiritual] leaders and submit to them [recognizing their authority over you], for they are keeping watch over your souls and continually guarding your spiritual welfare as those who will give an account [of their stewardship of you]. Let them do this with joy and not with grief and groans, for this would be of no benefit to you.*

Now, based on this verse, the role of the spiritual parent is to have the spiritual ability to keep watch over your soul. The word "watch" means to oversee, tend, or guard, especially for protection or safekeeping. It also means to keep under close attentive view or continuous observation for the purpose of seeing or discovering something. So, the spiritual parent must be able to oversee your soul. They must be able to see, observe, examine, survey, inspect, direct, supervise, and manage your soul from a higher position. Another word for oversee is the word "shepherd," which first and foremost refers to Jesus and the fact that He also shepherds through others that He has given the grace to operate in this position. A shepherd is a person who protects, guides, and watches over a person or group of people. Sounds like a parent, right? And they are to parent your soul.

The soul is the spirit part of humans. It is not visible to the natural human eye. It is the emotional part of the human nature. It is the seat of feelings and thoughts that initiate actions. The soul consists of the mind, emotions, conscience, and will of an individual. A spiritual parent must be able to see you beyond your physical appearance.

They should be able to accurately see your true spiritual condition, beyond what you want everyone else to see! If you are their spiritual daughter, they should have a balanced insight concerning you. They should correctly discern you with ease; the good, the bad, and the downright ugly concerning you. They should have and operate in the grace to see you for who you really are.

Many people think the spiritual parent's job is limited to imparting or activating some spiritual gifting, calling, or title, but the truth of the matter is that automatically comes as they birth your soul to a higher standard of living and operation. It is spiritually out of order to be more concerned about your giftings and callings than the condition of your soul. Why? Because you can be gifted and lose your mind! You can answer your calling and be emotionally unstable. You can be doing ministry and backslide. That's why it's important that both parties accept their position and role, because it is vital to your spiritual health and well-being.

It is a problem when you can deceive and manipulate your spiritual parent. It is also a problem when the spiritual parent has hang-ups that cause their discernment to be off concerning you. If your spiritual parent inaccurately discerns the condition of your soul then they will inaccurately discern your spiritual giftings, callings, and timing of the Lord for your life.

Now, of course God plays a major role in this for mistakes and such when individuals have a pure heart towards Him and others. He knows how to take up the slack. Especially where the flesh and carnality are concerned! I want to say this, the Lord will not withhold good from those who walk upright before Him (Psalm 84:11). Suppose that you as a spiritual daughter are walking honestly in accord with righteousness and your spiritual parents, for whatever reason, lack in giving you the things that are due to you for your proper growth, development, and well-being. God will not withhold any good thing from you. He will make sure you are supplied. I know that this is true from experience. The same applies when the spiritual parent is walking upright before the Lord. He will not withhold any good thing from them if the spiritual children are not doing their part. I have experience from this position, as well. He shall supply the need.

It was also mentioned in Hebrews 13:17 that we are to obey our spiritual leaders and submit to their authority. This is where the term "spiritual covering" comes into play. It is the spiritual authority that God has allotted them that has the power to protect the spiritual children they oversee. Their authority is the power God has given them to govern and have rulership. This is based on the measure of how God have found them faithful governing themselves, their lives, and the things of God. God must entrust them with the ability to govern and rule over the lives of others. The spiritual parents maintain that ability to cover through their obedience to God. This is what makes their prayers for you effective.

Now, you maintain being covered by their authority by being obedient and submitting to their authority until God causes authority to be passed on to you. This is how you gain authority, by respecting God's authority on your spiritual leaders. If your spiritual leaders are correct about spiritual matters and you make it difficult to receive them as a source of spiritual influence, advice, guidance, or information, etc., then it will also be difficult for you to receive authority to operate in the spirit realm. This is where it comes in about not making their job to cover you grievous. When this happens for a substantial amount of time, then you no longer reap the benefits of their covering, meaning that spiritual warfare that you were once protected from will be able to touch your life. It's as if the hedge of protection lifts.

Of course, you will still experience things in life, but proper spiritual covering is beneficial. God will allow certain things to humble us, grow us, mature us, etc., but not to allow the enemy to wreak havoc with us to the point of overtaking us for the enemy's gain. Ephesians 6:1-3 (NIV) says: *⁶ As for children, obey your parents in the Lord, because it is right. ² The commandment Honor your father and mother is the first one with a promise attached: ³ so that things will go well for you, and you will live for a long time in the land.*

Now notice this not only said to obey your parents in the Lord but to honor them. With honor comes the promise of things going well for you and long life in the land. This is major! When you honor them, this means you show a high respect for their rank in the spirit. This is when you have come to the place to recognize the difference of being covered by them versus not being covered by them. You notice the benefits of being covered and are grateful and feel privileged. You show them respect privately and publicly because of your gratitude for their authority covering your life. Most times, when I hear people quote Ephesians 6 they go straight to the part that talks about being dressed in the armor of God. But what I have come to realize is that before you can begin to put that armor on and be properly dressed for battle, you must be operating in the first three verses I mentioned above. If the root of obedience and honor was not established for your spiritual parents, then the spiritual armor mentioned in the rest of the chapter will not be in place. You will not be properly dressed spiritually with the authority to defeat the wiles of the devil.

Now, that word "honor" also means to manifest integrity in one's beliefs and actions. So, when you live, move, and have your being in the spiritual belief system that your spiritual parents birth you in, this brings honor to the name of the Lord and them. Yes! You honor them when you live holy and righteous. You honor them by living in integrity in your life, calling, and spirituality. This is a step beyond honoring them with your words, but with the way you live your life in their presence but more so in their absence. With this type of honor for God, first and foremost, and your spiritual parents comes the promise for things to go well with you and long life. This means for things to go well pertaining to your life and godliness. This means spiritually and everything that comes into fruition from the Spirit. It shall go well, and it shall live long!

Now, no spiritual parent or leader should be making you do things that are inappropriate. No spiritual parents or spiritual children should be pimping or hustling one another. Neither party should be entertaining inappropriate relations of any kind with one another that God has not ordained. Holy living should be the standard and the goal for both positions.

There are various things that should take place throughout the relationship that is developing with our spiritual parents. During this process, there should be a respect for God's anointed being established. As we are being covered by their authority in God, we should also gain a respect for the anointing on their life. To be acknowledged as God's anointed, we must first learn to respect His anointing on someone else. This begins with our spiritual parents. To respect the anointing, we must first give acknowledgement to the anointing in their lives. To acknowledge it means to recognize that it exists; that it's true and real. It also means to show and express appreciation and gratitude for it. When you truly acknowledge that anointing, you not only take notice of it, but you approve of it, you accept it, agree with it, support it, respond to it, endorse it, and defend it. This is what I call the Respect Factor, where you hold your spiritual parents in high esteem because of their spiritual worth and ability to birth you forth in God and the things of God. It is extremely important, because how you handle God's anointed will determine how you're handled as God's anointed. When God has placed His anointing on individuals and set them apart for a particular office, assignment, mission, task, etc., we must hold them in high regard and respect.

Psalm 105:15 (NKJV) reads: *15 Saying, "Do not touch My anointed ones, and do My prophets no harm."*

So, the Lord says not to touch His anointed ones. The word "touch" means to come in contact with, to come up to, to reach, to attain equality with, to compare with, to handle. In other words, He is saying do not try to be equal with them. Do not compare yourself to them. You must be careful how you approach them and handle them. This is serious because I have seen the repercussions of those who have mishandled God's anointed. It is not a pretty sight. I have seen people who toil in life and ministry because of this. They have mishandled someone who was anointed by God for real and then try to be anointed themselves and are extremely mishandled. I have watched those people fight tooth and nail to be respected in their calling and ministry with no positive results. I have seen people's lives in turmoil when this goes unrectified.

You must respect the person who is in real life anointed by God, whether you like them or not. And whether they like you or not. The best depiction of this concept is found in the account of Saul and David in 1 Samuel 24:4-20 (NKJV):

> *4 Then the men of David said to him, "This is the day of which the Lord said to you, 'Behold, I will deliver your enemy into your hand, that you may do to him as it seems good to you.'" And David arose and secretly cut off a corner of Saul's robe. 5 Now it happened afterward that David's heart troubled him because he had cut Saul's robe. 6 And he said to his men, "The Lord forbid that I should do this thing to my master, the Lord's anointed, to stretch out my hand against him, seeing he is the anointed of the Lord." 7 So David restrained his servants with these words, and did not allow them to rise against Saul. And Saul got up from the cave and went on his way. 8 David also arose afterward, went out of the cave, and called out to Saul, saying, "My lord the king!" And when Saul looked behind him, David stooped with his face to the earth, and bowed down. 9 And David said to Saul: "Why do you listen to the words of men who say, 'Indeed David seeks your harm'? 10 Look, this day your eyes have seen that the Lord delivered you today into my hand*

in the cave, and someone urged me to kill you. But my eye spared you, and I said, 'I will not stretch out my hand against my lord, for he is the Lord's anointed.' [11] Moreover, my father, see! Yes, see the corner of your robe in my hand! For in that I cut off the corner of your robe, and did not kill you, know and see that there is neither evil nor rebellion in my hand, and I have not sinned against you. Yet you hunt my life to take it. [12] Let the Lord judge between you and me, and let the Lord avenge me on you. But my hand shall not be against you. [13] As the proverb of the ancients says, 'Wickedness proceeds from the wicked.' But my hand shall not be against you. [14] After whom has the king of Israel come out? Whom do you pursue? A dead dog? A flea? [15] Therefore let the Lord be judge, and judge between you and me, and see and plead my case, and deliver me out of your hand." [16] So it was, when David had finished speaking these words to Saul, that Saul said, "Is this your voice, my son David?" And Saul lifted his voice and wept. [17] Then he said to David: "You are more righteous than I; for you have rewarded me with good, whereas I have rewarded you with evil. [18] And you have shown this day how you have dealt well with me; for when the Lord delivered me into your hand, you did not kill me. [19] For if a man finds his enemy, will he let him get away safely? Therefore, may the Lord reward you with good for what you have done to me this day. [20] And now I know indeed that you shall surely be king, and that the kingdom of Israel shall be established in your hand.

So here was David, who had been anointed by the Prophet Samuel to be next in line to become king. And King Saul was jealous of David to the point of trying to kill him. But notice that David never equaled himself with Saul by trying to kill him back. David acknowledged the fact that Saul was God's anointed and that he would not touch him. David understood the respect factor. And take notice of the fact that David addressed Saul as his father in this passage and that Saul addressed David as his son. King Saul is the person who God used to prepare David for the position as king. Regardless of how crazy Saul acted, it was up to David to maintain respect for him because God had anointed him. All the awful things Saul put David through equipped him to become one of the most powerful and well-rounded kings to ever live. It prepared David for all that God knew he would have to face in his time of reign. And because David respected King Saul and did not touch him, no one was able to touch or defeat David while he was in the position. David refused to mishandle God's anointed, even though God's anointed had hang ups that caused him to mistreat David. God anointed King Saul, so God dealt with him. The anointing David received to become the next king was activated by him serving under King Saul's leadership respectfully. That anointing empowered David to be able to endure that entire process blamelessly.

This was the Word of the Lord that empowered me to complete my own process blamelessly. The anointing in my life enabled me to uphold the Respect Factor while I was being processed into my position. The mistreatment seemed endless and too heavy to bear, but the anointing I walk in is weightier than all I endured. And this is the thing, nobody gets away. King Saul did not just get away with all the turmoil he took David through out of his jealousy. Once David's process was done, God dealt with Saul severely. And for the record, it was God who did not allow King Saul the opportunity to actually kill David. David always escaped. God gave David the opportunity to kill King Saul and David did not take it. So, no one was able to conquer and kill David throughout his entire reign as king. Nothing that came against David was able to prevail against him. Why? Because David successfully completed his process as a spiritual son under the leadership of God's anointed King Saul. By this, David received the training, preparation, respect, and authority necessary for him to function as king.

Many people are trying to operate in their callings without establishing the Respect Factor prior to functioning in their position. Without this, there is no real personal authority to operate in a spiritual office, position, assignment, etc. Now, every spiritual parent may not be as crazy as King Saul, but there are some who are. Your objective is to complete your process as a spiritual daughter as blamelessly as possible and receive all the equipping and preparation necessary to walk in your calling and favor with the Lord once He releases you to function. And it's also a blessing if you're able to maintain a healthy relationship with your spiritual parents after the grooming process is completed. Whether the relationship is tight or just cordial, just remain respectful. If anger, bitterness, unforgiveness, resentment, or anything arises at any time during the process, try to rectify it quickly. Pray, repent, and ask for forgiveness when necessary. Yes, we make mistakes, especially when we lack understanding of concepts, but it's best to be sincere and learn to resolve issues. And I mean to the point that God is pleased by how you handled the issue. I know this concept because I had to live it. When I made it to the end of that phase of my process and was getting ready to be ordained in the office of a prophet, the Lord gave me this verse of scripture as my reward. Proverbs 16:7 (NKJV) says: *When a man's ways please the Lord, He makes even his enemies to be at peace with him.*

This verse was a manifestation of all the lies, disappointment, and pain endured; a lifestyle of peace in return for all that warfare. God is faithful!

Queendom Quote

"The woman who understands order knows she must fulfill her role as a princess (daughter of faith) before she's able to discharge her duties as a queen (woman of God)!"

NATASHA OQUENDO

LET'S PRAY...

Father, I thank You for being perfect in all Your ways!
Forgive me if I have disrespected the
order You've set in place!
Forgive me for mishandling or trying to
bypass my position as a daughter!
Allow me to redeem any time I may have lost!
Enable me to receive all spiritual equipment
I may have missed!
Sensitize me to those who are truly filled with
Your Holy Spirit and wise counsel whom You have
assigned to my life!
Open the eyes of my understanding and enlighten me
to the importance and hidden treasures found
within my posture as a daughter!
I decree life to every part of my process!
Lord, enable me to redeem the time in any
part of my process I may have aborted
prematurely as a daughter of the faith!
I yield to Your perfect will for my life!
In Jesus name! Amen!

6ᵀᴴ KEY

DEVELOP
FAITHFULNESS

The Art of Serving

The Gift

One of the most cherished gifts honored by God, and humanity for that matter, is to possess the heart and ability to serve. To the point, the Bible says that the greatest among you will be your servant (Matthew 23:11).

One of the key components to the healthy development of becoming a spiritual daughter is to be processed by way of serving. To serve means to perform duties or services for another person or organization. It also means to be of use in achieving or satisfying a purpose. When we really take a good look, we will notice that serving is a major requirement necessary to function productively in this life. We are required to serve in every entity!

The fundamentals to becoming a servant begins in our homes. This foundation follows us into every other entity of our lives, causing us to offer our service in a variety of ways. Although serving in our homes is the beginning, we advance into schools, work force, businesses, public/community service, armed service, etc., and yes, even the church. As a spiritual daughter, it is much like the foundation that begins in our homes except it begins in the house of God. Serving God in His house is the foundation that prepares us to go out into the world to serve Him. By serving, we cultivate the powerful gift to give of ourselves symbolically, much like Jesus gave of Himself to serve us.

Think about it, Jesus gave His life for our sins so that we would be saved. Now that He has given us this example to follow, we are able to emulate His pattern of living by serving. One of the most important things to know about serving is that it flows from the posture of our heart. We must learn to serve out of a pure heart, a positive mind, and a good attitude. Much like the Bible calls for each of us to be a cheerful giver, we must be willing to serve in the areas where we're needed cheerfully.

THE MARY & MARTHA EFFECT

I have come to understand that we must accurately discern the posture he has placed us in to serve Him in each season of our walk with the Lord. The word "posture" means the way in which one is placed, arranged, or positioned. The best depiction of this is found in Luke 10:38-42, and it reads:

> *38 Now it happened as they went that He entered a certain village; and a certain woman named Martha welcomed Him into her house. 39 And she had a sister called Mary, who also sat at Jesus' feet and heard His word. 40 But Martha was distracted with much serving, and she approached Him and said, "Lord, do You not care that my sister has left me to serve alone? Therefore, tell her to help me." 41 And Jesus answered and said to her, "Martha, Martha, you are worried and troubled about many things. 42 But one thing is needed, and Mary has chosen that good part, which will not be taken away from her."*

First, I want to begin by saying that both Mary and Martha's posture of serving are two legitimate positions. In our walk with the Lord, we will experience them both. I believe the posture that Mary exemplified should be the posture of serving that we should begin with. Verse 39 says she sat at his feet and heard his words. This is a legitimate position in which we are to serve God. Sitting at His feet is a sign of humbling ourselves before Him. It is a position that symbolizes prayer, worship, and a low place for the Word to be poured into us. This is a posture where we receive the strength to stand to our feet and serve Jesus. In verse 42, Jesus confirms that this posture is needful, and that Mary had chosen the good part of serving Him which would not be taken away from her. This should be the foundation of which we begin to serve the Lord; in the posture of worship, prayer, and subjecting ourselves to the Word of God is how a firm foundation is laid.

When this foundation is properly laid in our lives, it will not be taken away from us! It is in this humble posture where our true soul work begins. Philippians 2:12-13 in the NLT reads:

> *12 Dear friends, you always followed my instructions when I was with you. And now that I am away, it is even more important. Work hard to show the results of your salvation, obeying God with deep reverence and fear. 13 For God is working in you, giving you the desire and the power to do what pleases him.*

So, we cannot take this posture of sitting at Jesus' feet for granted because it is the position that grounds us in our salvation and prepares us for the posture that Martha exemplified. And listen, there are many challenges that will come to keep you from getting what Jesus called the "good part" that came from Mary being postured at His feet.

Let me share my experience with this. I remember when the Lord had me postured in the Mary position, at His feet. The Lord pulled me to this posture and literally shut my entire life down. I was unable to find a job in that season. I mean, even the jobs that I was overqualified for would not hire me. I tried to enroll into school and was denied for the student loan. Those conditions forced me to consume myself in worship, prayer, and sitting under the Word of God. I could not understand for the life of me what the problem was. I was a very independent woman who was used to bringing in my own money; good money at that. During that time, I was completely humbled down to a pulp, and my husband financially took care of everything. I cried out to the Lord in prayer, and I heard Him say, "I shut the door!" I was only able to seek Him.

Now mind you, I did not fully understand why the Lord was allowing this. I continued to seek His face and obey the things He was confronting in my life. The reason that I'm sharing this is because some very interesting things happened while I was in this position. He had me in the posture of Mary, at His feet, and He completely shut my life down to make it possible. Now, while I was going through this process things got weird, and it came from those who were close and those who were familiar with me. Relatives, friends, and church family all began to talk about me and view me negatively. Many people around me did not, I repeat DID NOT, understand the posture that God had me in. People were saying things like they had never known me to be so lazy. Statements like, "That is not of God for her not to work and help her husband."

During that time, I even got false prophecies. Yep! You heard me right. People were giving me false prophecies. Someone told me that God said, "You need to get a job."

Now, this word didn't come from a random individual, this came from someone I respected. I remember that horrible feeling and going home crying out to God repeatedly; fasting and praying and hearing God say to me, "Natasha, I have shut that door!"

I even had an individual who fellowshipped at a different church than me come to my house and give me a strong rebuke. She said the Lord told her I was in error. That I needed to get a job and help my husband. She said I was being lazy and had not put any real effort into finding work. She prayed with me that day to find a job. While she was praying her prayer for me to find work, I heard the Lord clearly say to me, "Natasha, I shut that door!"

I didn't share with her what the Lord spoke to me because it finally dawned on me that there must have been a reason why He was not revealing His decision about me not working to them. So, I began to just accept the posture God had placed me in. I stopped allowing what people were saying about me to affect me. I took on another part of the definition of posture that focuses on the attitude a person has toward a subject. I shifted into a positive attitude about my position, because I came to realize that through all that confusion I was hearing His voice! I shifted my focus from all the negativity people were saying and focused on all the powerful things God was doing in and through my life. Once I decided to gain peace and make the most of my posture, the Lord allowed another sister in the Lord to confirm what He said to me. I was at church one Sunday, and as we were passing each other in the hallway, we hugged and she said, "I hear the Lord saying that you have been trying to find work, but God says He shut that door!"

I got weak in her arms like a limp noodle (lol)! She looked me straight in my eyes and said, "Look God is doing a work in you. Let Him do it! It doesn't matter who don't like it."

Then she prayed with me that God would complete His work in my life. Whew!

That encounter was a refreshing not because I felt it was something I wanted to hear, but because it was accurate. I can honestly say I'm not one who dwells on the person or even the delivery of the prophecy, I just want it to be an accurate word from the Lord, period. Now, this was my experience, and I am aware that not everyone will have the same experience but I'm sharing more so for the concept. I shared my experience to show how important it is to protect and respect the posture that God places you in.

Sitting at the feet of Jesus may not be easy or even desirable, but it is vital if you're going to last in the Martha stage of putting your hands to a work to serve Him. I can honestly say that I am so glad I surrendered to posture myself at the feet of Jesus and allow Him to do His work in me, my attitude, and some of my ways because I would have failed a lot of the tests that came while I was in the posture of Martha serving alongside some others in the church. I can be real, sitting at His feet has helped me not to fight. And trust me, I came close, but I didn't fight lol! I'm being transparent about the seriousness of sitting at His feet like Mary and how it prepares you for the battles that come with serving in the posture of Martha, which is hands-on, because if you're not delivered to an extent, you will quit.

And let me briefly share this: As for the individuals who gave me those inaccurate prophecies during my time of sitting at His feet, I held no issue whatsoever with them. I just understand that God did not reveal to them what He was doing with my life. And that is perfectly okay. Now, I did notice something very interesting. We must be careful as believers when God Himself places someone in a specific posture to serve Him that we don't speak a word to them that is contrary to what He is doing in their lives.

First off, such false direction can and has thrown people's lives into confusion, wrong timing, and out of God's will. Secondly, if we speak or judge someone's situation out of emotion, personal intellect, ill motives, selfishness, etc., there is a risk of being tried by our own words. I say this because in that season when God shut my life down, the person who came and strongly rebuked me about not working and helping my husband winded up not working, having to depend on her husband, and crying out to God. She had a very hard time during that season. I never said anything to discourage her about that season of her life, and I'm not sure whether she noticed what took place, but I did. I saw it but I concealed the matter and just supported her through it. I marked that occurrence for my own personal learning.

I also noticed a similar scenario with the other person who said, "God said you need to get a job!" For many years they have had to work a full-time job while trying to do ministry full-time. Now, I'm not saying anything is wrong with this position. But I do know that this is a lot to maintain. The point I'm making is that I learned that we must be careful when God has His hands on someone's life, working His will in them, to either be prophetically accurate or be quiet, because your own words can come back to test you to see if you're able to stand under them. Now, do I believe a sincere repentance and apology could have alleviated their outcomes? Maybe so. But I don't believe they even noticed or discerned what took place. I will say this, by the grace of God I am grateful that I didn't need any of those apologies or acknowledgments to move forward into my new level in my walk with the Lord. And that grace, my dear, came from spending time in the posture of Mary, at His feet!

As for the posture of Martha. This is the posture where you begin to put your hands on an assignment or a work. What I know is that first adequate time must be spent at the feet of Jesus developing that intimate love relationship with Him before you are properly equipped for this posture of Martha. When enough time has been invested in the work at His feet, then He enables you to stand in an assignment and experience the works of your hands being blessed. Your hands should be graced for every assignment you touch. You should have what they call the "Midas touch;" Everything you touch should turn to gold.

When you become a part of a work it should experience some form of increase. This is very important because this is how you start to identify the things God has graced you to do versus what you may just have a desire to do. For example, when I was the house prophet and head intercessor in my home church, the church experienced an increase in members and finances. The people increased spiritually and in the natural. Now, I did not say that everybody liked me, because they did not. But what I am saying is that God's grace showed up in my life in the areas that He assigned for me to do His work. So, this was not predicated on being the most popular or most well-spoken of. No! This was based on the principle of being postured at His feet long enough to get His blessing on the works of my hands and maintaining it.

I have seen when people put their hands to the things of God or have been in areas of His work not assigned to them, and they caused a complete mess. This happens because they have not invested enough time postured at the feet of Jesus and allowed Him to do a deep enough work in them equivalent to the assignment they are trying to engage. You must stay at His feet until He tweaks your attitude, mannerisms, temperament, personality issues, etc. Because these are some of the areas that will be tried and tested when it's time to do a work. I have literally seen people who have a destructive spirit with everything they put their hand to. Every idea they come up with never comes to fruition. Nothing they start ever really flourishes, reaches increase, or maintains manifestation. Many people are experiencing these things and lack understanding as to why.

I do want to say this. Hypothetically speaking, suppose you are praying, worshipping, sitting under the teaching of the Word, and serving consistently and are still experiencing the things that I described above. This could be an indication that you are more caught up with doing the act of these things than what they are supposed to produce in you personally. This could mean you are going through the motions, but your soul is not changing, because we prosper as our souls prosper (3 John 1:2).

Listen, there will be times when you're postured at His feet (Mary) and there will be times when you're postured working (Martha), and various times when you vacillate both postures simultaneously. The fact of the matter is that trying to do the work without spending the allotted time at His feet and doing the soul work is like driving your car to a destination and running out of gas well before you can get there. Basically, you won't have enough power to bring the work to completion. Neither the patience, character, healthy energy, or mindset to uphold the work. You want to be like Mary and choose the good part, because that intimate posture in Him will not be taken away from you. This is the posture where He blesses your heart, hands, and life to do the work. Remember, faith (Mary) without works (Martha) is dead (James 2:17). We must truly allow God to posture us in faith (Mary) so we can be productive in our work (Martha)!

SERVE THE LORD, WHERE?

There have been diverse perspectives concerning where we should serve the Lord. So, I want to make this as understandable as possible. The very first place that our service to the Lord begins is in the "Temple". Now, much of the definition of the word temple refers to a particular building devoted to administering sacred ordinances to a deity, principally that of eternal marriage. I want to focus on the part of the definition that says, "any place or object in which God dwells."

Let's look at 1 Corinthians 6:19-20 (NKJV): *¹⁹ Or do you not know that your body is the temple of the Holy Spirit who is in you, whom you have from God, and you are not your own? ²⁰ For you were bought at a price; therefore, glorify God in your body and in your spirit, which are God's.*

As we look at this verse it refers to our body as the temple. Our body in its entirety is the foundation of our service to the Lord! The work of service begins with our body, which houses our spirit and soul. Once we have accepted Salvation, God does a spiritual work with our spirit. We are responsible for the work on our soul and physical body, with God's help, of course.

Philippians 2:12-13 (NIV) states: *12 Therefore, my dear friends, as you have always obeyed—not only in my presence, but now much more in my absence—continue to work out your salvation with fear and trembling, 13 for it is God who works in you to will and to act to fulfill his good purpose.*

Remember I mentioned that Jesus came to seek and save what was lost, which was our soul? Our soul consists of our mind, will, emotions, and conscience. These are in a battle to align with the work God is doing with our spirit. Then, as our soul is coming into alignment with our spirit, it is our soul that causes our body to come into alignment. This work is accomplished through the posture of Mary, which is humbling ourselves and listening to the teaching of God's word, obeying His word, and developing a lifestyle of worship and prayer. When these things are put into action correctly and consistently, they tend to transform and elevate the condition of our soul. By this the soul becomes mindful of the condition of the physical body.

The soul work deals with mental health; emotional health and stability; the clearing of the conscience from present, past, and childhood trauma; and the alignment of the human will with the moral standards and ethics of God. Then there's the physical work that pertains to the body's health and well-being, giving it the strength and capacity to serve.

3 John 1:2 reads: *2 Beloved, I pray that you may prosper in all things and be in health, just as your soul prospers.* This is how we are to serve the temple of the Lord. It is in this measure of ongoing work that enables us to get fit and stay fit for the other avenues of the Lord's service.

Often, we may question where the best place is to truly be accounted for as serving the Lord. So, I believe the next best place to expound about serving the Lord would be in His sanctuary. This concept is found in 2 Chronicles 30:8-9, which reads:

⁸ Do not be stiff-necked, as your ancestors were; submit to the Lord. Come to his sanctuary, which he has consecrated forever. Serve the Lord your God, so that his fierce anger will turn away from you. ⁹ If you return to the Lord, then your fellow Israelites and your children will be shown compassion by their captors and will return to this land, for the Lord your God is gracious and compassionate. He will not turn his face from you if you return to him.

The word "sanctuary" is considered a sacred or holy place, temple, or church. The church is a public facility where worship and religious service is offered to God. It even says that the sanctuary is the part of the church that contains the high altar. Now, according to these verses of scripture, there were some very powerful benefits that came along with serving God in His sanctuary. Not only does God's anger turn away from the individual who serves Him in His sanctuary, but He also shows compassion to those connected to that person. Whew! I'm almost certain it is for this reason that Joshua stated, "As for me and my house we shall serve the Lord!"

This is how the blessing of the Lord is kept within bloodlines and maintained throughout generations by those who remain planted in Christ and serve Him in the capacity He has assigned them within His sanctuary. As I continue in the importance of serving God within His sanctuary, let me share examples of what I have noticed as added benefits to this principle.

I remember when I was growing up, I had to clean up a lot. This is what you could call a natural talent. I always received compliments on how clean my home looked and smelled. There was a time when the church I served in relocated and I offered to clean the bathrooms of the church free of charge. The Holy Spirit moved me to serve in this capacity and I noticed the need for it. I would purchase and bring my own cleaning supplies with no desire to ask the church for anything in return. I just remember being excited to offer my service. I would get down on my hands and knees to clean the floors with a sponge just like I did my floors at home. And the Lord would meet me there and speak to me like clockwork. I would praise, pray, and worship Him while I was cleaning those bathrooms twice a week. I cleaned them after bible study and after intercessory prayer. I remember feeling so good about being able to supply a need in God's house, but of course, as with anything it came with its challenges. People began to complain to the pastors about the bathrooms a lot! So much so that it seemed abnormal. I couldn't believe it because I am very meticulous with whatever I put my hands to do. I did everything in a spirit of excellence, so I couldn't understand for the life of me what the problem was. But, I can say that God causes all things to work out for our good. I sowed my service to clean into the house of God on my own dime. I was also led to clean a couple of the members' houses for free. The Lord allowed me to get some contracts to clean some very upscale houses. I made some very decent money during that season! Due to the quality of my work, word of mouth began to grow my business. It became too much for me to handle and I began to back off from expanding the business because I did not want the responsibility at that time of hiring people. I only wanted what I could handle by myself at that time, but I know the potential for that business would have been major.

My point is this, I know it was birthed because I served in God's house with my talent. I gave that service whole-heartedly, as if I was serving God Himself, and He caused it to multiply and become a resource for myself and my household to benefit from. It was because of this pattern that most things that I've operated in became successful. I'm sharing this because many people do not understand the blessing in serving in God's sanctuary, and that the services extend way beyond just preaching and teaching. The blessing comes from serving where there is a need in God's house, not where we desire to position ourselves to serve.

Can I tell you, there was a line of people waiting to grab the microphone to preach, pray, and prophesy openly, but no wait time for someone to clean the bathrooms, and it was needed. Do you know how filthy public restrooms can be? There was not a line of people for this work of service because the majority were and still are too prideful to perform this humble service with gladness.

I have so many examples of this concept, but I will just share one more. The Holy Spirit drew me into the place of personal prayer. Now mind you, this process I'm sharing took place over a span of a few years. Remember, I told you that the Lord shut my life down to take on this service. He assigned me to pray in His presence every day, and I mean for hours. I consistently spent time in His presence, and that is not an easy task. He must give you the grace and discipline to do this. And trust me, I know both sides of the coin very well. I know what it feels like to not be able to spend time in His presence in this capacity. So, it is a privilege if He enables you to do so. I spent that time in prayer, repenting and praying for Him to deliver me. I prayed for family, friends, and even strangers He led me to lift up in prayer. This was a daily routine. I have literally been found faithful within all the prayer watches (lol). I have accumulated many notebooks from God speaking and have experienced various supernatural encounters and divine visitations in the presence of the Lord. I know that these things were genuinely from the Lord because they were very humbling experiences. I'm sharing in depth because I want to reveal the power of this process when you offer your pure service to God and how He causes increase.

As I was found faithful in my assignment to seek the Lord's face, one Sunday during church my pastor said to me out of the blue that the Lord wanted me to head up the intercessory prayer for the church. There was no prayer ministry at the church during that time; everyone pretty much freelanced with prayer. Remember, I said the blessing is in when you are assigned to serve Him in the area of need! So, I obeyed the word of the Lord and began to head up the intercessory prayer ministry at the church. I decided to have it on Saturdays at 7 a.m. to prepare the atmosphere for Sunday services. Just a side note; you know my heart was sincere towards God to do this service as a young woman in my twenties every Saturday! Now, who does that? The sacrifice was real, but it didn't feel like a sacrifice at all.

At any rate, many of those Saturday mornings the Lord would wake me up very early to get to the church between 5 and 6 a.m. to prepare the atmosphere before the people would get there at 7 a.m. And, mind you, I had twin daughters who were toddlers at the time, so I packed them breakfast, lunch, snacks, Dora the Explorer sleeping bags, and VHS videos to occupy them in the children's classroom until prayer was over. Now, the powerful thing throughout that season was that they would literally stay asleep until the end of prayer. I was amazed at how God consistently did this to accommodate my service to Him.

After intercessory prayer, we would go to eat and then go evangelizing. Because my daughters were twins, they automatically drew attention, and they would give people the flyers and we would invite them to church. We came up with the flyers and printed them out on our own dime! God would move mightily while we out evangelizing. Now, to my point about increase, as I was faithful in my service to the need of the sanctuary, God began to bring my family and loved ones into salvation! It was literally like a domino effect. This goes back to the verses of scripture I shared from 2 Chronicles 30:8-9.

Now, I would be crazy if I didn't bring a balance to this and tell you that this assignment was extremely challenging. I watched people come and go. There were people who would come to prayer with totally wrong motives. People would come to spy and go back to report lies and all type of foolishness. I was amazed at the level of warfare that came with this assignment of service, but I stayed the course. Saturday intercessory prayer was for the members of the church, but the Lord had me to add the third Tuesday night of every month, which was open to the public. I did this until He released me from it.

One weekend I went to visit my hometown and left someone in a position to head up intercessory prayer for me. During my visit to my hometown, the Lord laid a burden on me for the city. The vision He gave me for a city-wide prayer crusade came to me while I was there. I contacted my pastor and told him what the Lord ministered to me. Now mind you, I tried to find a place to have this event in Atlanta where I was living at the time, but nothing was coming together for it to happen there. My pastor gave me his approval, and the Lord led me to the Panama City Marina, which was in the heart of the city. I was granted favor to have the prayer crusade in that location annually for seven years for free! I met with the mayor at that time, and she agreed to come and speak a few words at the event, which brought the news station on the scene, as well. Now, remember I told you before that some form of challenge and opposition came with these assignments, but previous process prepared me. I printed and mailed out flyers to all the local churches in the city inviting them to connect and be a part of the event to pray for the city. I paid for everything out of my pocket.

To my surprise, the greatest rejection came from the churches. I was floored! I could not understand for the life of me how the mayor agreed to be a part of the event and even declared it to be done annually, but the churches rejected it. I spent hundreds of dollars on flyers, envelopes, stamps, etc. to get their involvement. So, I went back and forth before the event and visited housing projects, homeless shelters, chemical addition recovery centers, etc. to invite them to the prayer event. This was based on Luke 14:23 (NKJV): And the Lord said to the servant, go out into the highways and hedges, and compel them to come in, that my house may be filled.

There was such a powerful move of God at this event. I created a platform to pray and release the word of the Lord over the city.

People led prayer, worshipped in song, danced, and released scripture, gospel rap, and poetry. The event was such a success that the mayor declared it at annual gathering. So, I hosted that event free of charge for seven years at that same location until the Lord released me. I also hosted a city-wide prayer crusade in three other cities. In each location I was granted favor. At that seventh year crusade, the Lord released me from that assignment and gave me the assignment to build a house of prayer for all nations in the city where we now reside, and I have purchased land in which we are waiting to begin the building phase of our effort.

I want to bring attention to a few key points in me sharing my testimony. I served God whole-heartedly in His sanctuary under anointed leadership with my gift to pray. I remained faithful to the assignment through the good, bad, and downright ugly. The Lord not only gave me the strength and favor to do the spiritual work, but He expanded the scope of my spiritual work. Now, I must be transparent and say that I wanted so desperately for the church to accept what the Lord was doing and join me in the work. I desired them to be in place to minister to those people who were being delivered after I left because I was still living in another state. I wanted them to be able to bring those people into the house of God and nurture the seed that had been planted. I didn't care whose church it was. At that time, none of those things were a factor to me only the souls of the people. Then various church goers began to gradually come out to be a part of this powerful move of God. Many of those who attended churches that came to that event experienced the activation of their spiritual gifts and various ministries were birthed forth in that atmosphere.

I hate to even have to say this, but it was once the churches began to get involved that things began to get crazy (lol)! Many of them came to spy out this event that they were hearing about that was so powerful in the city. They spied it out to copy and mimic the event. And I mean this literally. One lady I allowed to be a prayer minister in the event turned around thirty days later and had a prayer event at the same location and invited me to be a prayer minister. It was a struggle, but I humbled myself and participated and I will say this: God has a powerful way of showing exactly who the assignment truly belongs to. These are only a few of the many challenges that came with this assignment. There were a few church goers that went about spreading lies and rumors about me to many of the local pastors in the area with the agenda to stop them from connecting with me and attending to join the work. Now, I know this sounds just horrible, but remember, I had been thoroughly processed and prepared for this assignment.

Very similar things took place on a smaller scale when I was the head intercessor in my home church. So, when these things began to take place, I was able to continue in my assignment, obey the Lord, and bring it to completion because I had seen this before! It was to a greater degree but the exact same challenges! And God provided a greater authority, anointing, and grace for the task! It was for this reason, though the process at the time did not feel good at all, but it was necessary so that I would be fully equipped and prepared to serve the Lord at that level. The Bible says in 2 Corinthians 2:11 that, *"We are not ignorant to Satan's devices."*

I have so many more powerful testimonies I could share on just how misunderstood the assignment of serving God in His sanctuary really is. The natural talents and spiritual giftings you dedicate to serving in God's sanctuary with, out of a pure heart, a right spirit, and enduring the process, can literally birth you into potential businesses, ministries, and positions. I gave two examples, one of a natural talent that birthed into a business and a spiritual gift that birthed into a ministry. Now this may not be the extent of results for everybody because many things come into play, like the will of God for your life, the extent of your willingness to process and obey the Lord, the giftings and talents you possess, etc. But for the most part you shall experience some form of increase by investing yourself to serve in the sanctuary!

So, lets address the importance of being planted in the church that God wants you to be in to do your acts of service. This may not necessarily mean where it's most comfortable or convenient for you. From my experience, I have observed most people choose the sanctuary they want to fellowship in based on fleshly desires and feelings of sensualism. If they like good singing, they go because of the praise team or the choir. They may choose a church based on their children's department. Another reason is because the pastor or church is famous. Then, maybe because they have acceptance issues, they attend for acceptance and social belonging. Then there is the reason by way of their family grew up attending the church. I have seen people attend various churches for the reason of finding their mate. Some go because they are attracted to the pastor. These are just a few of the many reasons that people choose a church to attend. Though these reasons may sound legitimate, they are not accurate. The first reason should be because that is where God wants you to be. Someone might ask, "How do I know this is where God wants me to be?"

There are a few factors that come into play in order to know. You want to be at a church where the power of God to bring the repentance that leads to salvation is operating. You want pastors who actually live a holy life to the best of their ability. You also want the message that is preached to locate you in your sins and bring you to a place of conviction consistently. This one is important because without conviction and challenge to change, there is no real growth within as a child of God. You will grow in your knowledge of the Word but not in the power to live the Word; and the power of the

Holy Spirit that brings healing and deliverance is added value to that church.

Now, I shared this because the churches that have these manifestations may not be what feels or appears comfortable or convenient for that matter. But for the most part, this is the type of church that you want to serve in. Here is a very good reason as to why we need to serve in the Lord's sanctuary. 2 Chronicles 30:8 states: *⁸ Now do not be stiff-necked, as your fathers were, but yield yourselves to the Lord; and enter His sanctuary, which He has sanctified forever, and serve the Lord your God, that the fierceness of His wrath may turn away from you.*

The Bible tells us to enter the Lord's sanctuary to serve Him! Serving Him in this way turns His wrath, which is His anger, away from our lives. This wrath turns away because truly serving Him in His sanctuary is developing us into His royal priesthood. 1 Peter 2:9 (NKJV) reads: *but you are a chosen generation, a royal priesthood, a holy nation, His own special people, that you may proclaim the praises of Him who called you out of darkness into His marvelous light.*

To be chosen by God for the work within the sanctuary is an honor to not be taken lightly, for granted, or mishandled. The priesthood is being set apart as a priest to serve God by handling religious duties, and requirements, and to offering sacrifices that God will accept. The sanctuary or church is where you learn how to handle what God has declared sacred. The church is where things and people are considered holy. At least they should be. This part is vital because how this part of the process is handled can determine whether you live in blessings or curses. Through the process of the priesthood, you're learning how to respect God, how to handle what's sacred, and how you should maneuver to please God.

This is why temple work, which is the work on self, is so important. The lack of in-depth temple work will cause you to mishandle sanctuary work and holy people. The mindset when operating within the house of God should be as though it's literally being done for God Himself. Because it really is! If the church you're serving in and the leadership truly belong to God, that is. This goes for everything you do within the church. From cleaning it to serving in the pulpit, all aspects must be well respected and handled with complete care. As the priesthood, you learn to offer God every aspect of You. You are investing your time, talent, money, etc. into a spiritual inheritance that is eternal. Sacrificing yourself to prayer, fasting from sin, and holy living creates an eternal pathway for your bloodline. This process is not a quick one, because it is eternalizing you. This is why the entire mindset about the church and what it's all about must shift. The church is the entranceway and preparation for God and His use.

Let me put it like this: we are to serve in the church until we are filled with the Holy Spirit to advance to the work of the Kingdom. Luke 24:49 says: *Behold, I send the Promise of My Father upon you; but tarry in the city of Jerusalem until you are endued with power from on high.*

That promise from the Father was the Holy Spirit. The word "tarry" means to wait for, to stay, or remain in place. We must remain in the church until we are empowered by the Holy Spirit to effectively perform the work of the Kingdom, which is out into all the world.

Another area of serving the Lord is within His Holy Kingdom. You graduate to this level of serving after you have processed to being filled with the Holy Spirit and have learned to be led by and operate in the Holy Spirit. Luke 17:21 (NKJV) says: *21 nor will they say, 'See here!' or 'See there!' For indeed, the kingdom of God is within you.*

This represents a way of life that is governed by the Holy Spirit dwelling inside of you. He is at work guiding and leading you in the will, way, and work of the Lord. This is the ability to live holy outside of the walls of the church. This is you having the ability to navigate in holiness within the nations and cause the nations to expand in holiness. 1 Peter 2:9 (NKJV) reads: *but you are a chosen*

generation, a royal priesthood, a holy nation, His own special people, that
you may proclaim the praises of Him who called you out of darkness into
His marvelous light.

This scripture identifies us as chosen out of our generation to become royal priests and ultimately a holy nation of people. The word "kingdom" means a state or government having a king or queen as its head. The Kingdom is the domain which the spiritual sovereignty of God or Christ extends whether in heaven or earth. Although you respect and abide by the world's systems, time frames, and laws, you as a Holy Kingdom citizen are not bound by them where the will of God is concerned because you have learned to maneuver everywhere with what is sacred respectfully. You can serve the True and Living God while living in this world without deviating to serve the other gods of this world. By this, we have been given a mandate so that this way of holy living is multiplied. This mandate is found in Matthew 28:18-20 (NIV):

> *[18] Then Jesus came to them and said, "All authority in heaven and*
> *on earth has been given to me. [19] Therefore go and make disciples*
> *of all nations, baptizing them in the name of the Father and of the*
> *Son and of the Holy Spirit, [20] and teaching them to obey everything*
> *I have commanded you. And surely, I am with you always, to the*
> *very end of the age.*

In simple terms, the Kingdom work will be everything you do outside of the demographic of the church that has the potential to make followers of Christ. This is your life in navigation with Christ's agenda as your ultimate purpose being fulfilled in whatsoever you put your hands to do. This is people seeing and experiencing the Kingdom of God in operation outside of a church service. As a representative of the Kingdom of God, the Holy Spirit has the liberty to reach who the Lord has willed through your life.

Now, I have given the condensed version of these three areas of serving the Lord. Each part of these processes is extensive and takes time. There are no magical fixes; this is real life. But for the most part, the work of the temple, the work of the sanctuary, and the work of the kingdom are our areas of service unto God.

WHY SERVE THE LORD?

There are various reasons why many people serve the Lord. I believe some of the main reasons should be because of our love for Him and to enter Heaven. I also shared from 2 Chronicles 30:8-9 that as we serve the Lord, His anger turns away from us and He shows compassion to our children. These are some very powerful reasons to serve Him, and I want to go into a few more.

There is an amazing opportunity that takes place within the process of development as a spiritual daughter. We get a chance to "Redeem the Time!" This means you get a chance to do something good to compensate for poor past performance or behavior. Let's take a look at Ephesians 5:14-17, which says:

> *14 Therefore He says: "Awake, you who sleep, arise from the dead, And Christ will give you light." 15 See then that you walk circumspectly, not as fools but as wise, 16 redeeming the time, because the days are evil. 17 Therefore do not be unwise but understand what the will of the Lord is.*

Once we are awakened to the saving power of Christ, it is an opportunity to vindicate our position as a daughter. Maybe you were a rebellious child? Of course, most of us made some bad choices as daughters to our natural parents in some form or fashion, but there is an opportunity to get a do-over! Yes, as a spiritual daughter who serves the Lord, there is a chance to make amends for the sin, errors, and evil committed as a natural daughter. Along with this opportunity, we must be mindful not to become repeat offenders by serving the Lord with a rebellious spirit. If rebellion ruled, you as a daughter in the natural then you should be careful not to allow those same mindsets and actions to transition into your life as a spiritual daughter. Be mindful, because if you're not vigilant the same negative actions can play out in your spiritual walk. The time spent serving God in holiness redeems all the time that was spent entertaining evil. We begin to build up an account in the Spirit that leads to a spiritual inheritance and legacy for our bloodline. By sincerely serving the Lord and redeeming the time, generational curses begin to be broken over your life and the lives of those connected to you. I am a living witness to the power of God in this. Many of my family members have gotten saved and are now serving and living in the favor of the Lord! Serving the Lord is filled with benefits, and it also has its challenges.

I have come to realize a few things during this journey that I believe will be helpful. While the benefits of serving God are wonderful, I think it's best to bring a balance and be made aware that there are enemies to serving. Now, I've noticed that as we first come into salvation, many of the enemies we will face will be the things we were bound by before salvation. For instance, one of my personal battles was my temper. I had a very bad temper that had a stronghold on my life because not only was it a generational curse, but it was fueled by traumatic life experiences. Now, I was never one to start any trouble or drama. I tried hard to stay away from people who entertained drama because I did not do well with it. I had always had an extreme mindset when it came to protecting myself, and I can admit that it may have been not only extreme but dysfunctional. So, I spent majority of my beginning stages wrestling in prayer and fasting with this enemy. Not only that, but many challenges came to test my deliverance in this area.

For the most part, I tried to avoid the people that I knew could cause that side of me to rise from the dead (lol)! I could spot people who had bully spirits and started drama from a mile away, so I stayed away from them; not because I feared them but because I feared not being able to control myself. Plus, I wanted to please the Lord. Besides, I put in a lot of work to be delivered.

Now, have I gotten angry? Of course. The Bible says to be angry but not to sin or let the sun go down on our wrath (Ephesians 4:26). I used this as an example to say that in your beginning stages, you will wrestle with your personal stronghold. Whether it was fornicating, committing adultery, stealing, lying, cussing, fighting, etc., those enemies will try you while you're in your process. Now, those may be the enemies of your inner self, meaning things you may battle with within yourself. But I noticed a few enemies that followed me into the church. I remember speaking to my first lady when I first came into the church, and as I was telling her about things I had been through, she began to prophetically tell me that the spirits of jealousy and envy would follow me into my salvation. I just remember feeling so disappointed because I had expected things to be different once I got saved and into the church. I had dealt with a lot of rejection due to people being jealous and envious while I was a sinner, so I was truly looking forward to not having to deal with any of that in the church, or so I thought.

I'm sharing about the enemy of jealousy because this was the enemy that tried to run me out of the church and cause me to stop serving God altogether. This enemy posed as a real threat to me completing my process as a spiritual daughter.

The word "jealousy" means to have resentment against a person enjoying success or advantage, etc., or against another's success or advantage itself. Now, from my extensive experience of this spirit fighting against my life, I have noticed that it gives plays to a murdering spirit, a lying spirit, and the spirit of sabotage. That spirit tried to murder my reputation and credibility in ministry before I even began! You see, while I was being processed through serving and developing as a spiritual daughter, I was falsely viewed as if I was developing an ungodly relationship with my pastor. Now mind you, my pastor is about the exact same age as my natural father. I was never the type of female who liked much older men. Nothing against anyone else's preference, but I thought that was disgusting when men old enough to be my father tried to make advances towards me. Furthermore, I have been stalked by older men a few times as a teenager. So hopefully you catch my drift.

This false accusation came about somewhat privately, then progressed to an outright public platform. I was approached privately and told that I pulled on my pastor too much and that it did not feel right. Now, I was in a very fearful season of my saved life because I began to have supernatural encounters and visitations with the Lord, and other members I tried to confide in about these things were not having things of this nature happening in their lives, so this caused a disruption among the congregation. I was a member of a small church, and because others were not having these types of encounters, I was viewed as the power of God on my life being a demonic power instead of the real deal. God was birthing His deliverance ministry in my life. In other words, I began to operate in the power to cast out devils. The incident that caused this disruption was when the Lord used me to cast the spirit of drug addiction out of someone in my living room (I will share that person and their testimony at some point but not now).

Well, after the deliverance took place, I noticed that the fish in my aquarium were acting crazy. They were swimming upside down and swimming into the big rock and into the glass of the tank. Any time I walked by the tank, they would jump up and hit the top of the tank; one even flipped out of the back where the filter was. The fish were literally trying to kill themselves! The young lady who first invited me to the church came by my house and I explained to her what happened, and she saw the fish for herself. She laughed and said, "I have never seen anything like this, but it's in the Bible."

She read about when Jesus cast out the legion of demons and they went into the pigs and the pigs ran into the water and drowned themselves. This was just one of many real-life examples that I can share. My pastor told me to share the encounters only with him because many of the congregants were not able to receive my experiences. I shared these things with him because honestly, I was afraid and wanted to be certain that these things were legitimately of the Lord and not a demonic spirit. I wanted accountability to know that I didn't tap into a demonic realm. My heart was pure in my confiding in him for guidance; first and foremost because he told me to. I earnestly viewed him as a father figure in my life, and I believe he had my best interest at heart. I also believe his dealings with me were pure, as well. He did nothing inappropriate towards me, and vice versa, so it was to my amazement when I was approached privately. I was instructed not to mention this to anyone, not even my husband.

Now, this thing sent me into a spiritual turmoil that I can't begin to explain. I felt like the situation knocked me into a spiritual coma. I remember going into prayer repeatedly in extreme turmoil, gaining a temporary peace but no relief. Now, this was the private approach that knocked the absolute wind out of me. But it didn't stop there. The public part came as an open humiliation. At a church anniversary, there was a woman pastor whose ministry was covered by my pastors, and she preached her entire message against me without saying my name. In her message, there were a lot of things that indicated that she was referring to me, but the statement I want to highlight was when she said, "That's a shame, you got your own husband but want the pastor!"

Now, the crazy thing was that I stayed through that entire service with tears running down my face and my hands lifted worshipping the Lord. At the end, my pastor spoke, choked up and almost in tears. He said, "If you are still here, I know it's because you really love the Lord."

Other people knew the message was about me because there were a select few who tried to speak life into me and encourage me. I can be honest; I went through a few different emotions. When I went home, I cried and then I got angry! The more I thought about it, the more I wanted to really snap and go back to my old ways. I broke down and went into prayer, and I can remember saying to God that "Lord this stuff is a lie! That's just not me!"

I wrestled in prayer until all my strength left me and I laid limp. The presence of the Lord was on me so heavy that I could not move. That's when He began to speak to me. He said, "Natasha My truth lives in you. That truth will not only stand but will outlive the lies. You will not run. You will not leave. The anointing I've placed on your life is weightier than any trial you will ever face. Now, stand still and see My salvation!"

I was in my prayer closet and fell asleep in His presence until the next day. He gave me the strength I needed to endure that season without becoming bitter. I gave this as a condensed version because there was a lot that went along with this, but I shared this not for the details but more so the principle. This was the enemy that tried to rob me of my identity and inheritance as a spiritual daughter! The point is I had to fight a good, hard fight in faith to complete my process. I know many who have aborted their process for way less.

Now, I know someone may be saying, "That was not of God! You didn't have to put up with that! I would have left! You had every right to leave!"

And all these may be true. But I am so blessed that God enabled me to obey Him. Believe it or not, but this stuff prepared me to become unstoppable in every assignment. It showed me how to submit to the will of God in my life regardless of fleshly and emotional desires. The very enemy that was meant to cause me to abort my process actually drove me to a place in prayer and the presence of God that I would not have been able to enter into with everything going well.

Though at the time it seemed so unnecessary, I have seen these types of things throughout my walk with the Lord. For example, some would not invite me to speak because of jealousy and intimidation issues. Just know that there are some people who do not know how to handle attractive people in the world or in the church. From my experience, some beautiful women become the enemy not because they do something wrong but because some women feel that their husbands, or the men they are with, will find that woman attractive. Now, this was one of my main enemies, but I have seen many types in the lives of women as they process to becoming a spiritual daughter. And for the record, by God's grace I still have a relationship with my pastors. I was licensed, ordained, and released into the work of ministry by them. This is why perception means everything. It can become one of our greatest enemies to serving as a spiritual daughter.

Perception is how you perceive or apprehend with your mind and senses. It is how we understand and comprehend things. The wrong perception of spiritual things can throw everything off. For example, let me look at my scenario from the flip side. I've seen women who were attracted to their pastor for real and vice versa. They view the man or woman of God as someone common and not someone who houses their spiritual inheritance. It is dangerous for a spiritual daughter to view the father in the spirit as a husband, date, or sex partner because it forfeits the position as a spiritual daughter and all the benefits that come with it. This is a spiritual act of incest!

Another enemy I've noticed is being too prideful to be a daughter. There are women who feel like "I'm grown!" They perceive themselves from the natural standpoint and never even attempt to enter the realm of a spiritual daughter for many reasons. They may be too familiar with their leadership. They may be related to them, grew up in church with them, or maybe they're friends and don't have the respect necessary to receive them as leaders. I have also seen women forfeit their process by a counterfeit showing up in their lives, especially when they have embraced celibacy, the desire to live holy, and save themselves for marriage. The counterfeit shows up when they are making spiritual progress but are desperate for a man. Desperation is when you become reckless or dangerous in your decision making due to feelings of despair, hopelessness, or an urgent need or desire.

This desperation is not just by happenstance, but it is a consequence that is found in scripture. Genesis 3:16 (NKJV) reads: *16 To the woman He said: "I will greatly multiply your sorrow and your conception; In pain you shall bring forth children; Your desire shall be for your husband, and he shall rule over you."*

The desire for a husband and that desire ruling the life of women is the consequence of the woman's sin in the garden. The manifestation of this consequence lives on to this day through the lives of women. Most times that desperation is fueled by a wrong motive for a significant other. The lust for sex hiding as loneliness. A desire for financial help in the household. Wanting help with children. Competing with others. Whatever the case, it is the lustful motive that draws the counterfeit.

Now, the counterfeit can show up as a person from your past reaching out to you, or a completely new individual but with the same spirit as a person from your past. I also want to mention that the counterfeit will lure a woman away from her God-given assignment. The man the Lord sends will not come against your God-given assignment. I have seen women choose a man over God and the things of God too many times to count. Who God sends will be complimentary to everything God has assigned and how He has positioned you. The counterfeit will be more compatible to the fleshly and carnal nature, but not spiritually. The main reason the counterfeit or any other enemy shows up is to divert you from receiving and developing the fruit of submission that comes from completing your process as a spiritual daughter!

QUEENDOM QUOTE

"The powerful woman offers her best service in every opportunity knowing that God keeps the most accurate account!"

NATASHA OQUENDO

LET'S PRAY...

Thank You Lord for being the most
powerful example of a servant!
If I have ever served You with a wrong mindset,
attitude, or motives please forgive me!
Grant me the grace to serve You cheerfully
with my whole heart!
Empower me to please You!
Provide me with the strength and
faithfulness to serve!
I appreciate every opportunity to serve You!
Clothe my life to represent You well!
Let my service flow out of my love for
You and your people!
Saturate me in the oil of gladness that
others may desire to serve You, too!
I praise You for keeping an accurate
account of my service!
I believe that my reward comes from You!
I love You Jesus!
Amen!

7TH KEY

ADJUST TO THE REALM!

YOU MAY ENTER

THE ENTRANCE: SUBMISSION

It was about 10:00 a.m. on a beautiful spring Sunday morning. I was so excited as we were on our way to church, enjoying the ride as we listened to heart-felt worship music. The sound of singing and laughter filled the car as I keyed in on the gorgeous flowers in full bloom along the way. In good spirit and great expectation, I strolled into the church doors hungry for the word of the Lord that would strengthen and carry me for the week. Intercessory prayer was powerful and filled with the presence of the Lord. My spirit was ready. Then suddenly, one of the assistant pastors stepped to the platform and began to speak about wives submitting to their husbands. If I can be honest, the message came across as if it had a specific aim and motive. All the excitement I felt going into the church that morning took a downward plunge, that's for sure. But I still had hope, the message from the main service. To my surprise, the same message comes across, with my pastor shouting in a loud voice, "Wives submit!"

As I scanned the room, I saw every woman in the church was quiet with their heads held low, and some men were shouting "amen!"

I thought to myself "these messages seem personal." I mean, why not just have a conversation with your wives at home if you feel like they're not in submission to you? There was such a heaviness in the atmosphere. As a woman, I felt a bit beat up. And I know for a fact the other women in that service felt the same.

For the rest of the evening, I could not get the message out of my mind. It left me thinking to myself, "Am I submitted to my husband?" and "What does this submission entail?"

I had so many questions, and though the message seemed harsh in its delivery, it did ignite a desire to understand it better. I asked my husband what he thought about the message. He said it didn't come across as a problem we had because he felt as though I was submitted to him. I can honestly say I felt a sigh of relief with his answer, but I wanted to understand the concept more. After much prayer, study of scripture, and hearing the hearts of other women throughout the years, the Lord has revealed the much-needed understanding I desired. I can see clearly why the enemy would want to leave a bad taste in our mouths concerning submission. He wants us to feel like slaves and as if everyone means more than we do so that we'll miss the benefits of our submission.

I want to begin by saying that it is our fruit of submission that causes us to enter our queendom position. The submission gained while serving God in the posture of a daughter prepares and equips us for every assignment God has in store for our lives.

The word "submit" means to yield oneself to the power or authority of another. It means to be presented for the approval, judgment, opinion, or decision of another or others. It also means allowing oneself to be subjected to some kind of treatment, influence, or action. So, to say we are in submission is to yield our control over to a more powerful or authoritative entity. As women, we are required to submit to God, our husbands if we're married, and the authority figures in our lives. The reason for this is so we as women will have a sign of authority over our heads in the spirit realm. This is no different than the church, symbolic of the woman having to submit to Jesus to operate in the measure of authority that supersedes the natural world. In other words, the woman being submissive, which is her being compliant with the authority of God, her husband, and the leadership in her life grants her authority to operate in the spirit world and the natural world at the same time. This shows the spirit world that as a woman you're not operating in rebellion or disobedience with the order of God. When you are in right standing with both worlds you become a force to be reckoned with. Your ability to influence is now backed with God's authority. Your submission is vital to ensure your perpetual victory to accomplish everything you set your hand to do.

Your life bearing the fruit of submission not only gives you entrance into your queenly position, but it makes you a candidate to be a sub in the mission. To "sub" is to act or serve in place of another. Then you have the word "mission," which is to be sent for a duty or purpose. It also means any important task or duty that is assigned, allotted, or self-imposed. It is a goal, aim, assignment, purpose, calling, commission, duty, life work, job, operation, function, calling, office, business, or profession. This is why God calls us to and processes us through submission, because He wants us to be willingly obedient and easily manageable for the assignments He has purposed us for.

A great example of this can be found in Esther chapter 2. Throughout this chapter, there is a pattern of submission found operating in Esther's life. She submitted to her cousin Mordecai, who adopted her as his own daughter after the death of her parents. During that time, King Xerxes was looking for a new queen and Esther was in the running. The women were entrusted to the king's servant Hegai, with whom Esther, through her trail of submission, won his favor. Esther 2:15 reads: *When the turn came for Esther (the young woman Mordecai had adopted, the daughter of his uncle Abihail) to go to the king, she asked for nothing other than what Hegai, the king's eunuch who oversaw the harem, suggested. And Esther won the favor of everyone who saw her.*

Long story short, she followed his instructions and gained her position as queen, and ultimately fulfilled her purpose to bring deliverance to the Jews. She became the sub in God's mission to bring freedom to the Jews. It was her fruit of submission that caused her to not only stand out but to win favor throughout every part of her process into her position as queen. A woman who bears the fruit of submission becomes a powerful force in the hands of God to accomplish great and mighty exploits!

Now, to bring a much-needed balance to this topic, I want to say that you must use wisdom and good old common sense when dealing with various things you should submit to. First and foremost, things that go against the word of God and the will of God for your life don't warrant your submission. Not to say that God won't allow you to endure uncomfortable situations and circumstances, because He will. But in instances that threaten your life and overall wellbeing, be wise. In things that risk your salvation or holiness, be sober. The situation where I was falsely accused of wanting my pastor in a way that was not proper wasn't life threatening, but it was challenging. I stayed the course, because God said to do so, and I experienced the victory. Time and integrity not only healed the wounds but tested and proved noble character. Submission to the will of the Lord for your life places you in the position for God to defend and protect you.

THE BEAUTY: PURIFICATION

Beauty, beauty, beauty. The theme of the day. One of the popular topics of our times. A subject full of diversity, pain, and mystery. Yet, an attribute most desired among women. The topic of beauty looms so weighty in our atmosphere, constantly molding us into the mindset that our physical beauty determines our worth. Now, there is some truth to this, but not the whole truth. Let's explore it.

The word "beauty" means a combination of qualities, such as shape, color, or form, that pleases the senses, especially the sight. It is the pleasing or attractive features of something. It is also considered the best feature or advantage of something. In the definition we can obviously see that physical beauty is pleasing to the human sight. But in the sight of God, it is a different story. Proverbs 31:30 (NIV) says: *Charm is deceptive and beauty fleeting, but a woman who fears the Lord is to be praised.*

That word "fleeting" means to last for a very short time. So physical beauty has a time limit on it and we find ourselves trying to fight back the hands of time. Regardless of the magnitude of physical beauty we possess, time happens to us all. This makes me think about how God makes everything beautiful in His time (Ecclesiastes 3:11). In this, God reveals that the beauty that He's concerned with takes time to develop. This beauty is much deeper than mere physical appearance, but is instead a queendom beauty that reaches beyond the physical surface and enters the very core of our existence.

I believe that true beauty is an inside job with an outward expression. This beauty transcends the human experience into eternity. Let's look at God's definition of beauty, found in 1 Peter 3:3-4 (NKJV), which reads" *3 Do not let your adornment be merely outward—arranging the hair, wearing gold, or putting on fine apparel— 4 rather let it be the hidden person of the heart, with the incorruptible beauty of a gentle and quiet spirit, which is very precious in the sight of God.*

The passage identifies this as an incorruptible beauty, which speaks of a beauty found in a woman's character that is strong enough to not be persuaded to do wrong. This speaks of a woman who is concerned with exemplifying high moral values. It even goes a step further and describes how that incorruptible beauty manifests itself in the woman's spirit in the sight of God. This beauty causes God to see the woman's spirit as gentle and quiet. Gentle meaning able to be easily handled or managed, and quiet meaning absent from noise. It also means to be free from disturbance, interruption, or the interference of others. It even means to reside in a peaceful or settled state.

In other words, this is a woman that God can easily guide and lead her life without her fighting against His will for her. She is settled in her obedience to Him. She is at peace with God's decisions concerning her life. So, her spirit shows up in God's sight as gentle and quiet, but manifests in the earth realm as excellence of character. Now, I believe this is the perfect place to liberate you from a potential bondage. Notice the Lord said a quiet spirit, but not a quiet mouth. Because you can be quiet in speech, but your spirit be in a loud fight against the will of God for your life. If you give God the liberty to manage your spirit, then He can use your mouth to speak. The key is knowing when to speak a thing and how to say it. There is a grace of speech that comes with the incorruptible beauty He bestows on your life.

I want to take the time to share from the book of Esther, chapter 1, for just a bit. We have King Xerxes who throws this massive seven-day banquet in the third year of his reign. He is showing off the wealth and splendor of his kingdom. At the same time, his wife, Queen Vashti, is throwing a banquet for the women in the royal palace, as well. On the seventh day, while the king's heart was merry from drinking wine, he commanded his chamberlains to bring his wife Queen Vashti before him with her royal crown to show the people her beauty, and she refused to come. Her reaction angered the king, and he sought advice from the wise men who knew the times and understood the kingdom's laws. Ultimately, they made the decision to release her from her royal position and choose another woman as queen to replace her. This could be viewed as an extreme reaction, but let's look deeper into it.

Esther 1:15-20 (NIV) states:

> [15] *"According to law, what must be done to Queen Vashti?" he asked. "She has not obeyed the command of King Xerxes that the eunuchs*

have taken to her." ¹⁶ Then Memukan replied in the presence of the king and the nobles, "Queen Vashti has done wrong, not only against the king but also against all the nobles and the peoples of all the provinces of King Xerxes. ¹⁷ For the queen's conduct will become known to all the women, and so they will despise their husbands and say, 'King Xerxes commanded Queen Vashti to be brought before him, but she would not come.' ¹⁸ This very day the Persian and Median women of the nobility who have heard about the queen's conduct will respond to all the king's nobles in the same way. There will be no end of disrespect and discord. ¹⁹ "Therefore, if it pleases the king, let him issue a royal decree and let it be written in the laws of Persia and Media, which cannot be repealed, that Vashti is never again to enter the presence of King Xerxes. Also let the king give her royal position to someone else who is better than she. ²⁰ Then when the king's edict is proclaimed throughout all his vast realm, all the women will respect their husbands, from the least to the greatest."

The problem was not Queen Vashti's physical beauty, but more so the beauty of how she had to present herself in the position of a queen. Her physical beauty alone was not enough to sustain her in her position. She openly lost her fruit of submission. Remember, the fruit of submission was the entrance into the position and that fruit must be maintained. There was a more elegant way to handle that situation, but God had an extremely important mission to be fulfilled by Queen Vashti's replacement who possessed the fruit of submission and physical beauty that came from the inside out.

To better understand this beauty that comes from the inside out, let's look at Esther 2:12 (KJV) that reads:

Now when every maid's turn was come to go in to king Ahasuerus, after that she had been twelve months, according to the manner of the women, (for so were the days of their purifications accomplished, to wit, six months with oil of myrrh, and six months with sweet odors, and with other things for the purifying of the women).

There are other translations that call this process beauty treatments, preparations, and beautifications. For this reason, I wanted to show the linkage between the word beauty and purification. The beauty that transcends from the inside out is our purification. It is the purity of our heart, mind, and motives that affects our outward appearance. These are the things that remain in plain view in the sight of God but may not be accurately seen by others. The women were required to go through this purification process and beauty treatment for a total of twelve months before they were able to go before the king in an intimate way.

"Purification" is the act or process of making something pure and free from any contamination. It means to purify from anything that debases, which means to reduce or defile in quality, value, or rank. It also includes being purified from any foreign elements, such as something strange or unfamiliar in character or nature. It is the act or process of making something free of guilt or evil. Purification is also the act or process of making something clean and fit for ceremonial or ritual usage.

This element of beauty is the same for us as we take our rightful place as queens. One of the required oils used in that purification process was the "oil of myrrh" for six months. Myrrh is a sap-like substance that comes from trees. It is often used as a fragrance, to flavor food products, and for its potential health benefits. Biblically, myrrh was included as one of the gifts presented by the wise men after the birth of Jesus (Matthew 2:11). Then myrrh was also a part of the mixture brought for the preparation and burial of the body of Jesus (John 19:39). Myrrh was one of the principal spices used in making the sacred anointing oil (Exodus 30:23) and was also one of the key fragrances on the queen's royal robes (Psalm 45:8-9). The spice myrrh was not only an important ingredient from a spiritual standpoint, but also in its common use.

Myrrh was commonly used as an embalming oil for dead bodies. This makes me think about our process and how certain attributes we have within our makeup must die; the negative traits we possess that can hinder our growth, progress, and usage. 2 Corinthians 5:17 (NKJV) reads: *Therefore, if anyone is in Christ, he is a new creation; old things have passed away; behold, all things have become new.*

I believe that oil of myrrh symbolizes some of the new that has replaced the old things that have passed away in our lives. The oil of myrrh was commonly known for its healing properties, its ability to kill harmful bacteria, to fight fungal infections, help with blood circulation, boost the immune system, etc. It is also a very popular ingredient used in beauty products for the improvement of the skin. These details are being shared to make an important point about the topic of beauty. The women during the time of Esther were preparing themselves for the queendom position. They endured six months of purification with the oil of myrrh and six months of beautification with sweet odors. The oil of myrrh symbolizes the replacement of the old things that had to die and be buried in us, and the sweet odor represents the personality we must possess.

The word "sweet" means having the pleasant taste characteristic of sugar or honey; not salty, sour, or bitter. It also means (of air, water, or food) fresh, pure, and untainted. So symbolically, that sweetness is to replace any bitterness or saltiness you may have gained whether by way of generational curses or just plain old bad experiences in life. This purification is the beauty!

When your heart, mind, and motives have been purified, there is a beauty that emanates from the inside that shows up outwardly to the point that your physical appearance does not look like what you have been through. There is this beauty that shows up as an outward glow due to the purification that you're carrying within. It's just like going through a body detox or cleansing. The process may be a bit rough, but in the end, you not only feel better, but you look better. Likewise, is the beauty that comes from the purification of your spirit; an eternal beauty that transcends time!

THE SUPERPOWER: FAVOR

What is our real-life superpower as women? Well, when we think about the word "superpower," the first thing that comes to mind is a superhero. Yes. We think of those supernatural abilities that come with being a superhero. We tend to focus on whatever abilities we may have that make us appear in some way to be superhuman. Especially with being a woman, there is always this talk of a "woman's intuition." And of course, there's the ancient belief in women having the supernatural strength to give birth. Even in the realm of faith, we often think of the gifts of the Holy Spirit as our superpowers, with the gift of prophecy and various gifts of healing at the forefront of the list. These are all amazingly mind-blowing concepts that contain some truth and validity in nature. But there is more.

By way of definition, the word "superpower" means a very powerful and influential nation. It is a state which holds a dominant position possessing military or economic might, or both, characterized by its extensive ability to exert influence or project power on a global scale vastly superior to that of other states. When we look at the meaning of the word superpower, it makes us think about having some form of access and impact on a massive level. It speaks of being statewide, national, and global in reach. It makes you wonder, "What superpower do I have that equates to this massive level?" and, "How do I tap into this magnitude of superpower?"

At one point in time, these questions were very hard to answer, but now the world wide web has made things much more accessible.

Let's look beyond the obvious and grasp a greater understanding. I want to say that God Himself is the bigger and greater avenue that has complete access to the entire world. As women, it is our favor with God that is our superpower. You may wonder why I say this. I mean, it just seems way too simple, right? Let's explore it. "Favor" is the state of being approved or held in regard, preferential treatment, to aid or support, or to bear a physical resemblance to. So how does the superpower called "Favor with God" look in the life of a woman? How do we identify this approval, preferred treatment, or support from God? We will investigate the life of Mary the mother of Jesus.

Luke 1:26-38 (NKJV) says:

> *26 Now in the sixth month the angel Gabriel was sent by God to a city of Galilee named Nazareth, 27 to a virgin engaged to a man whose name was Joseph, of the house of David. The virgin's name was Mary. 28 And having come in, the angel said to her, "Rejoice, highly favored one, the Lord is with you; blessed are you among women!" 29 But when she saw him, she was troubled at his saying, and considered what manner of greeting this was. 30 Then the angel said to her, "Do not be afraid, Mary, for you have found favor with God. 31 And behold, you will conceive in your womb and bring forth a Son and shall call His name Jesus. 32 He will be great and will be called the Son of the Highest; and the Lord God will give Him the throne of His father David. 33 And He will reign over the house of Jacob forever, and of His kingdom there will be no end." 34 Then Mary said to the angel, "How can this be, since I do not know a man?" 35 And the angel answered and said to her, "The Holy Spirit will come upon you, and the power of the Highest will overshadow you; therefore, also, that Holy One who is to be born will be called the Son of God. 36 Now indeed, Elizabeth your relative has also conceived a son in her old age; and this is now the sixth month for her who was called barren. 37 For with*

God nothing will be impossible." [38] *Then Mary said, "Behold the maidservant of the Lord! Let it be to me according to your word." And the angel departed from her.*

In these verses, we see the angel of the Lord comes to Mary and says that she is highly favored by God and that God is with her. So why did the Lord choose to favor her? There are two important elements that stand out about Mary. The first thing we notice is her status as a virgin. From a literal sense she is a virgin, meaning she has never had sexual intercourse. So how does this apply to us? Because majority of us are not virgins from a literal perspective, but let's understand the spiritual perspective of this. Some of the synonyms for the word virgin are pure, uncorrupted, unpolluted, undefiled, chaste, moral, self-denying, and sinless, to name a few. These synonyms mirror the beauty of purification I discussed in the previous section of this chapter. Otherwise, most of us would be disqualified from obtaining favor with God. But the beauty that is developed from the process of purification grants us access.

The second element was the connection Mary had. She was engaged to Joseph, who was born in the bloodline of King David, which means she was connected to the Word that God promised to the bloodline of King David. To truly be connected to God's Word, which is a promise and prophecy, is to believe it to the point you'll obey it. Think about it, Mary was a believer in God's Word so much so that her belief caused her to maintain her purification. This concept is the same for us. We must believe God's Word and allow it to process us through purification, knowing that the purification is a manifestation of our belief in God and His Word.

Now I want to highlight the benefits of finding your superpower (favor with God). Luke 1:30-31 (NIV) reads: *[30] But the angel said to her, "Do not be afraid, Mary; you have found favor with God. [31] You will conceive and give birth to a son, and you are to call him Jesus.*

In this, we find that she was given the power to conceive and give birth. Here was a word of promise given to Mary, and because of favor she was able to conceive the Word. For her that meant she was able to become physically pregnant with a son. But symbolically for us it means the part of the definition for the word "conceive" that means to form or devise a plan or idea in the mind. It also means to form a mental image, to imagine, to envision, to grasp, to visualize, to see, to dream, to think, to develop, or to create. In other words, favor with God opens you up and empowers you to be a carrier of His vision concerning your life. You become a carrier of His word just like Mary.

Now, you are not limited to just being a carrier, but God Himself gives you the strength to give birth to what you have conceived. Birth is the act or process of bringing forth offspring. So, He makes sure that you experience the manifestation of what you have been given the ability to conceive. And furthermore, He obligates Himself to be with you. Because you are carrying His word, His plan, His vision, His seed, His purpose, His assignment, He in return is with you constantly, supporting you and causing your life to experience preferential treatment. This is your superpower!

Because you are favored, He keeps you as the apple of His eye (Psalms 17:8). He's not only with you and constantly watching over you, but He's causing your life to not fall. Psalm 46:5 (NIV) says: *God is within her, she will not fall; God will help her at break of day.*

This means He will constantly uphold you in your queenly position.

Look at what Psalm 41:11-12 reads: *[11] By this I know that You favor and delight in me, because my enemy does not triumph over me. [12] And as for me, You have upheld me in my integrity and set me in Your presence forever.*

Here, you can see this superpower called "favor" is active against every enemy in every way that would come to attack the integrity He has invested in you. Your integrity is important to God. He is concerned with you being able to maintain your moral principles, your uprightness before Him, your wholeness, and your unity with Him. He wants you to keep your internal consistency pure and sound. Why? Because He loves being with you! If you notice, Mary quickly agreed with the Word of the Lord the angel gave her. When we agree with His word and align ourselves with it, He obligates Himself to walk with us (Amos 3:3).

The superpower of favor causes you to become a valuable asset and a powerful force in various ways. For this reason, you must understand its value and learn how to navigate in it. When you have truly settled in your superpower, those who connect with you will experience the favor of the queendom realm you reside in. The reason this happens is that there has been an atmosphere created due to the Presence of the Lord. Remember, this favor with God is your superpower because He is with you. His Presence in your life is attractive, meaning many may be drawn to it. At the same time, His Presence in your life is intimidating, meaning many may also be warded away from it. This happens because those who enter into connection of some sort with your life must be beneficial to the purpose and plan of God concerning you. Because ultimately, your superpower of favor will be beneficial to their lives hands down. For this reason, you must trust God fully. He knows the motive of every individual you will encounter. It took me a while to understand this concept. God knows exactly who should be in affiliation with you, whether that means in close or from some distance. This is why our purification process is necessary. We must be delivered from the need to be accepted and the fear of being rejected.

When we feel the need to go out of our way the be accepted by individuals that God may have caused to reject us, then we set ourselves up to take on unnecessary mental and emotional damage. When you understand your superpower then you understand why certain relationships, connections, or situations may or may not be a good fit for your life. And you cannot expect everyone to celebrate your favor with God. There will be many who look on your favor in the spirit of jealousy, envy, and covetousness. It may cause some people to strive and compete against you. You must not engage in or entertain any of this activity, because your superpower has specific assignments that you must pay attention to. In other words, you cannot allow these things to become a distraction.

The journey into your superpower is a process that takes patience, because favor with God is birthed in stages. The best depiction of the stages of favor can be clearly seen in the life of Joseph. In Genesis 37:3-4 (KJV) we can see the beginning stage: *³ Now Israel loved Joseph more than all his children, because he was the son of his old age: and he made him a coat of many colors. ⁴ And when his brethren saw that their father loved him more than all his brethren, they hated him, and could not speak peaceably unto him.*

Here we see that Joseph gained the favor of his father, and with that favor came hate from his brothers. Now, did this seem fair to the other children? Maybe not, but this is the reality of what preferential treatment can potentially look like to those who may not experience it. Then Joseph has a few prophetic dreams that he shares with his family, and even his father rebukes him. The dream still mirrors Joseph in a preferred position, so this sparks envy in his brothers towards him (Genesis 37:11). Now notice that Joseph was able to conceive the dream from the Lord about his future, although no one else believed in it. So, Joseph began to experience hate, then envy, and at the opportune time his brothers conspired to throw him into a pit in order to divert his dream from coming to pass (Genesis 37:20). While in the pit, some merchants found him, and he was sold into slavery and taken to Egypt. Now even in this horrible situation Joseph's superpower was still in operation.

Genesis 39:2-5 (NIV) says:

² The Lord was with Joseph so that he prospered, and he lived in the house of his Egyptian master. ³ When his master saw that the Lord was with him and that the Lord gave him success in everything he did, ⁴ Joseph found favor in his eyes and became his attendant. Potiphar put him in charge of his household, and he entrusted to his care everything he owned. ⁵ From the time he put him in charge of his household and of all that he owned; the Lord blessed the household of the Egyptian because of Joseph. The blessing of the Lord was on everything Potiphar had, both in the house and in the field.

In this we see that Joseph, even as a slave, was experiencing favor with God, and those connected with him experienced the effects of his favor with God, as well. Now, this is superpower in operation! And just because your superpower is causing others to be blessed does not exempt you from being tested.

Genesis 39:7-10 (NIV) reads:

⁷ and after a while his master's wife took notice of Joseph and said, "Come to bed with me!" ⁸ But he refused. "With me in charge," he told her, "my master does not concern himself with anything in the house; everything he owns he has entrusted to my care. ⁹ No one is greater in this house than I am. My master has withheld nothing from me except you because you are his wife. How then could I do such a wicked thing and sin against God?" ¹⁰ And though she spoke to Joseph day after day, he refused to go to bed with her or even be with her.

This was a test of Joseph's integrity. His favor with God, meaning God was with him, empowered him to maintain his integrity. And though he made the right decision, his master's wife still falsely accused him because he would not sin against God by sleeping with her. Once she lied about him by falsely accusing him of trying to sleep with her, Joseph was put in prison where the king's prisoners were confined. And even in the prison, he experienced favor (Genesis 39:20-21). While he was confined with the king's prisoners, God caused the cupbearer of the king and the king's baker to have a dream. Joseph accurately interprets both of their dreams.

Now, I want to bring something very important to the light. As I mentioned before, your superpower of favor with God is taking you through a process that not only teaches you how to maintain your integrity so that your favor with Him remains intact, but it also develops and matures you in your spiritual gift. In the beginning of the process, Joseph had his own personal dreams, which he explained without a clear understanding. Then he was given the opportunity to hear the dream of others and give them a clear and accurate interpretation that came to pass. And just because his gift was powerful and accurate, it did not make the cup bearer remember him when he wanted him to. Why? Because his superpower had not finished processing him into the position God had ordained for him yet. He remained in prison two more years before the Lord caused the King Pharaoh to have a dream that no one could interpret. This situation caused the cupbearer to remember how Joseph gave an accurate interpretation of their dreams that came to pass. So, Pharaoh sent for Joseph. This is when Proverbs 18:16 (NKJV) comes into play, which says: *A man's gift makes room for him, and brings him before great men.*

While Joseph's superpower (favor) was processing him, there was room being made for his gift to be properly placed in the rightful position that God predestined for him. There was an appointed time for Joseph to be positioned. Joseph not only gave Pharaoh an accurate interpretation of his dreams from God, but he also gave him God's instructions on the solution for the famine that was coming. Because God was with Joseph and gave him wisdom to discern the times and instruction on what they should do, it caused Pharaoh to exalt Joseph into the position to be second in command.

Now, there were some awesome things that took place. Joseph was placed as second in command of all of Egypt. He was placed in royal attire and given gifts and rewards. And he was presented with a wife who was the daughter of a priest. Joseph thrived in his position, and amid the famine he was able to relocate his family and position his brothers to serve in the land of Goshen, where they experienced the realm of Joseph's favor with God. Joseph's superpower served a major purpose during a critical time.

There are a few things I want to reiterate. Your superpower is your favor with God. That favor takes you through a process that takes time to develop. During its development, there are various things that are taking place. You are learning how to maintain your integrity, which is your strong moral principles and unity with God because He is with you. In that process, your gifts are identified, cultivated, and matured. Remember, Joseph had giftings such as prophecy, dreams, interpretation of dreams, wisdom, discernment, and leadership. And please notice that although he possessed powerful prophetic giftings, he was not titled as a prophet, but those giftings were the equipment he needed to fulfill his God-ordained position as a governor.

I share this because we must be careful that we don't potentially get stuck in the process by taking on a calling that was only intended as a temporary placement to equip us for our true God-given position. There must be an undivided trust that God knows what's best for you and that His timing is perfect. Also, stay aware of the enemies of your process into fully functioning in your superpower. There will be those who hate you because God has favored you. The fact that you have tapped into your superpower will cause people to become jealous and envious of you. Because of your integrity, there will be some who feel like you are "too good to be true," so they will try to find fault with you. You cannot be surprised by false accusations, lies, or even sabotage. There will be those who outright reject you, and at the same time there will be those who desire to use you for their personal gain. These things are all a part of the process, not to destroy you but to activate your integrity with unstoppable power.

You must fight to remain full of the integrity that God invested in you and not become contaminated with bitterness or unforgiveness because of mistreatment. This is important because once you are truly positioned and functioning in your queendom realm, you will become a source of blessing not only to those who love and respect you but also to those who may have neglected, mistreated, and mishandled you.

Remember, you are blessed and highly favored among women! God is with you! Your focus is to conceive, carry, and give birth to His vision and purpose for your life. And last but definitely not least, let nothing and no one come between you obtaining and maintaining your superpower. The fact that He has favored you is fair.

THE STANDARD: VIRTUOUS

Now that you understand the importance of your superpower, which is your favor with God, let's look into maintaining that superpower. Everything in life that bears the existence of quality, importance, success, or value must adhere to a fundamental standard to be maintained. With a standard there are expectations and responsibilities that are involved. So, how does the standard apply to women of faith? What is the woman's responsibility in this standard? There are various meanings for the word "standard," but we are going to pull the part that means something set up and established by authority as a rule, custom, model, or example.

Based on this, we know that God is the authority and Christ is the ultimate model and example, but what is the specific custom for women? What is the main rule we must follow? How do we model or exemplify this standard? Well, the answer is found in Proverbs 31:10 (KJV) that says: *who can find a virtuous woman? for her price is far above rubies.*

This verse mentions a "virtuous woman" and it speaks of her as if she's hard to find. It even places her value to be far above rubies. And rubies are considered a rare stones. This implies that being a "virtuous woman" is not a popular thing, but rare. And virtuous is the standard that upholds your position in the queendom. So, what is virtuous? To be virtuous is to exhibit moral excellence in character and behavior. It speaks of conforming to moral and ethical principles. In other words, it is a behavior that shows high moral standards by doing what is right and avoiding what is wrong. We know that a virtuous woman is settled in her decision to walk with the Lord. She is not someone who is wavering between right and wrong; doing right has become a way of life for her.

There are some interesting aspects that I want to bring to the forefront of meeting the standard of becoming a virtuous woman. Proverbs 31:10-11 the NIV version says it like this: *10 A wife of noble character who can find? She is worth far more than rubies. 11 Her husband has full confidence in her and lacks nothing of value.*

This version calls a virtuous woman a wife, and not just a wife, but she is a wife who possesses noble character. Noble not only as in qualities that are honorable and admirable, but qualities that are high in rank. In other words, they are the qualities and characteristics of royalty. Queenly in nature, if you catch my drift?

Taking your rightful position in the queendom means you have entered through the gates of the nobles (Isaiah 13:2). Upon entering this royal position, you also enter into the spirit of a wife. Yes! The standard positions you spiritually as a wife and manifests in the earthly realm as a virtuous woman. Being virtuous means you are faithful in your union with God. Remember, God is with you! You and the Lord have become one. Having the spirit of a wife is what qualifies you for marriage in the natural realm. When you are in your proper position in the queendom, then the husband that God has for you can find you.

Remember, "a wife of noble character who can find?" It is her husband who truly finds her because he has located her spirit. Think about it. Proverbs 18:22 (NKJV) says: *He who finds a wife finds a good thing, And obtains favor from the Lord.* When the husband finds his wife, he obtains favor from the Lord. Why? Because the wife is not only maintaining a virtuous standard, but she is operating in her superpower which is favor with God. This causes him as her husband to experience all the good things God has instore for his life. Why? Because God is now with him and his wife. And now, a three-fold cord is not easily broken (Ecclesiastes 4:12).

You see, living in the standard is a powerful thing, because you become the prize! What's even more powerful is that you possess these qualities of a wife in the spirit realm even if you're not married in the natural realm. Yes! Being a virtuous woman makes you God's prized possession, and if you get married in the natural realm, you become your husband's reward. Look at Proverbs 12:4 (NKJV), which reads: *An excellent wife is the crown of her husband, But she who causes shame is like rottenness in his bones.*

This verse describes the virtuous woman/wife as a crown. A crown is a reward for victory or a mark of honor. It is also the royal headdress worn by a sovereign. So, can you see what's happening here? By being your husband's reward from God, you bring him to an elevated place of royalty. This is why it's so important to rightfully take your queendom position within the kingdom of God. By doing this, you come to a healthy place of truly understanding the value you hold in this world. This makes your process into your queendom position crucial. Being in your right position makes you an extreme benefit to all who are connected to your life. Maintaining your posture as a virtuous woman in the earth realm, which is a wife of noble character in the spirit realm, is your responsibility to the standard. This is your part. And God is so faithful that He has a powerful part that He fulfills.

In the midst of this wonderful journey, while you're upholding the standard of being virtuous, the Lord Himself is also helping to uphold the standard, as well. Being that God is the authority who has established the standard, He has obligated Himself to be an enemy to your enemies. The first enemy is the devil, of course. 1 Peter 5:8 (NIV) says: Be alert and of sober mind. Your enemy the devil prowls around like a roaring lion looking for someone to devour.

This means the devil does not have the permission or the authority to destroy you, because by being in your rightful position within the queendom, you are no longer within his reach. When the enemy attempts to come in like a flood, it is the Spirit of the Lord that lifts the standard against him (Isaiah 59:19). Think about it. The fact that you're operating in your destiny as a virtuous woman and have decided that obedience to the Lord's Word is what is right, then He magnifies your will to do right with His righteousness. God being with you empowers you to do right and builds up a resistance that combats the enemy coming against you. The devil may form weapons against you, but those weapons will not prosper in their outcome (Isaiah 54:17). Now, will things happen in your life? Of course they will, but you will not be destroyed. The Lord will not allow the devil to destroy you, neither will He allow you to self-destruct.

The best way to self-destruct as a woman of faith is to give your flesh control of your life. Yes. The works of the flesh operating in your life can prove to be more fatal than anything the enemy can bring against you. For this reason, God is an enemy to your two biggest enemies, the devil and your flesh. How? Well, the word "standard" also means an emblem, banner, or personal flag of the head of a state, a member of a royal family, or organization. Because God is with you and loves you, He becomes a banner over your life.

In your queendom position, God reveals Himself to you as Jehovah Nissi "the Lord is my banner." A banner symbolizes an important message. This message speaks of the certainty that God has granted true victory over the flesh. This symbolism is found in an ongoing battle between the Israelites and the Amalekites, much like the ongoing battle we have against our flesh. Historically, the Amalekites were birthed out of the lineage of Isaac's son Esau. And remember, Esau chose a pot of red meat over his birthright, which was symbolic of his spiritual inheritance. Not only that, but the pot of red meat represents the flesh. When Esau made this choice, the Bible said that God hated Esau (Romans 9:13). And when the Amalekites showed up to ambush the Israelites after they left being in bondage in Egypt, it angered the Lord (1 Samuel 15:2).

In this same way, it angers the Lord when we are headed to the place of blessing and favor in Him and we're ambushed by the flesh. Let's take a deeper look. Exodus 17:14-16 (NIV) reads:

> *14 Then the Lord said to Moses, "Write this on a scroll as something to be remembered and make sure that Joshua hears it, because I will completely blot out the name of Amalek from under heaven." 15 Moses built an altar and called it The Lord is my Banner. 16 He said, "Because hands were lifted up against the throne of the Lord, the Lord will be at war against the Amalekites from generation to generation."*

In this passage, we see where the Lord promises to completely blot out the name of Amalek, just as He promised to blot out our sins and remember them no more (Isaiah 43:25). Then Moses makes a declaration that the Lord is their Banner. He does this because they won the battle against the Amalekites, and the Lord promises to war against the Amalekites from generation to generation. God gave them the victory against the Amalekites while Moses kept his hands lifted before Him in a submitted position.

It is amazing to see that the battle is not yours, but the Lord's. He is consistently dedicated to helping you live your life in victory.

Knowing the Lord as your banner is the sign that your victory and triumph is inevitable. This is so comforting and encouraging to know that as a standard bearer within your queendom position, that God obligates Himself to uphold His part of the standard to ensure that you experience success in every area of your life.

The invitation to queendom is a formal and personal calling into your God-ordained identity and position within the kingdom of God. It is a realm of existence where God takes up partnership with every aspect of your life. In the queendom, you live your life with unlimited access to the power and authority of God. In this book, we have unpacked the fundamentals of the real-life process of not only getting into your queendom position but revealed the foundation of maintaining your position.

Once you enter into your realm through the fruit of submission and take on the beauty of your realm through purification, you unlock your superpower, which is the favor of God! And you maintain your realm by upholding the standard of being a virtuous woman. Now, don't think for one minute that this is all. No! This is only the beginning of an amazing journey to experience God in ways unimaginable! This realm is fully loaded with so much mystery, assignments, and rewards to unfold! God is with you! You shall not fail! Receive your "Invitation 2 Queendom," and let's navigate in excellence together! Your time is now!

QUEENDOM QUOTE

"The woman who has a vision considers nothing too hard in order to enter into the realm where all things are possible!"

NATASHA OQUENDO

LET'S PRAY...

Father in the name of Jesus!

I believe You have chosen me to reside and

operate in Your realm of favor!

Forgive me if I have fallen short of it in any way!

Give me the chance to develop the fruit of submission,

that I may enter into it!

Grant me the beauty of purification that comes

from Your Word and Your Presence!

Activate my superpower!

Let my life overflow with favor!

Empower me to function effortlessly in the spirit of a wife!

I decree and declare that I'm a virtuous

woman filled with faith!

I receive Your invitation to my queenly

position and true identity!

I decree, that I live in the realm where all things are possible!

Thank You for choosing me!

In Jesus name! Amen!

End Notes

All bible verses are from one of the following versions of the bible King James Version, New King James Version, New International Version, and New Living Translation.

Acknowledgments

To GOD be all the glory for what HE has done!

Author Bio

NATASHA OQUENDO is an enthusiastic transformational speaker; mentor; life/relationship coach; and conference, seminar, and workshop host/speaker. Driven by her passion for helping others reach their greatest potential, she started her career aiding people in need. This decision led her to speak and mentor persons in prisons, homeless shelters, chemical addiction recovery facilities, battered women's shelters, and high schools with troubled teens.

Apart from her work with crisis prevention and rehabilitation, she also inspires people in areas of work-life balance, self-help, entrepreneurship, and spiritual empowerment. She motivates people to access their true identity by helping them discover their aptitude and set realistic goals to achieve their fullest potential.

With a bachelor's degree in ministry, she is a licensed and ordained prophet currently pastoring at Flow of the Spirit International Ministries alongside her husband. She is the CEO of Powerful Life Institute, which has broadened her audience through all forms of virtual communication outlets, including television, radio, and written publications.

One of her greatest personal motivators is her family. As a wife and life partner to her husband and a mother to a set of adult twin daughters, she values down time with her family traveling, enjoying foreign cuisines, and the Floridian lifestyle of frequenting the beach. She credits her ability to balance being a CEO, life/relationship strategist, and now published author to the unconditional love and support of her family.

Made in the USA
Monee, IL
26 April 2023

32461657R00095